Adventures in New Guinea

James Chalmers

Alpha Editions

This Edition Published in 2021

ISBN: 9789354753008

Design and Setting By
Alpha Editions
www.alphaedis.com
Email – info@alphaedis.com

TABLE OF CONTENTS

INTRODUCTION

Public attention has been repeatedly and prominently directed to New Guinea during the last few months. The name often appears in our newspapers and missionary reports, and bids fair to take a somewhat prominent place in our blue-books. Yet very few general readers possess accurate information about the island itself, about the work of English missionaries there, or about the part New Guinea seems destined to play in Australian politics. Hence a brief sketch indicating the present state of knowledge on these points will be a fitting introduction to the narratives of exploration, of adventure, and of Christian work contained in this volume.

New Guinea, if we may take Australia as a continent, is the largest island in the world, being, roughly speaking, about 1400 miles long, and 490 broad at its widest point. Its northernmost coast nearly touches the equator, and its southernmost stretches down to 11° south latitude. Little more than the fringe or coastline of the island has been at all carefully explored, but it is known to possess magnificent mountain ranges, vast stretches of beautiful scenery, much land that is fruitful, even under native cultivation, and mighty rivers that take their rise far inland. Its savage inhabitants have aroused powerfully the interest and sympathy alike of Christian Polynesians and English missionaries, who, taking their lives in their hands, have, in not a few instances, laid them down in the effort to win New Guinea for Christ.

At some remote period of the past, New Guinea, in all probability, formed a part of Australia. Torres Strait itself is only about sixty miles wide; the water is shallow; shoals and reefs abound, giving the sailor who threads the intricate and dangerous navigation the impression that he is sailing over what was once solid earth.

The first European sailor who sighted the island was D'Abreu, in 1511; the honour of being first to land belongs most probably to the Portuguese explorer, Don Jorge De Meneses, in 1526, on his way from Malacca to the Moluccas.

Into the somewhat intricate history of the connection of the Dutch with the north-west coast of New Guinea we cannot here enter. As suzerain nominally under the Sultan of Tidore, they claim possession of the western part of the island as far east as Lat. 141° 47' E. The trade they carry on is said to be worth about 20,000*l*. a year. Dutch missionaries have for many years been stationed around the coast of Geelvink Bay.

In 1770, Captain Cook visited the south-west coast, and in 1775, an English officer, Forrest by name, spent some months on the north-east coast in search of spices. In 1793, New Guinea was annexed by two of the East India Company's commanders, and an island in Geelvink Bay, Manasvari by name, was for a time held by their troops.

Partial surveys of the south coast were made in 1845 by Captain Blackwood, who discovered the Fly River; by Lieutenant Yule, in 1846, who journeyed east as far as the island to which he has given his name; and in 1848 by Captain Owen Stanley, who made a fairly accurate survey of the south-east coast.

The most important survey work along the coast of New Guinea was done in 1873 by H.M. ship *Basilisk*, under the command of Captain Moresby. He discovered the now-famous harbour, Port Moresby; he laid down the true eastern coastline of the island, discovering the China Straits, and exploring the north-east coast as far west as Huon Gulf.

In many parts of the world Christian missionaries have been the first to get on friendly terms with the natives, and thus to pave the way for developing the resources of a savage country and leading its inhabitants in the paths of progress and civilization. Pre-eminently has this been the case in South-eastern New Guinea. White men had landed before them, it is true; but for the most part only to benefit themselves, and not unfrequently to murder the natives or to entrap them into slavery. Christianity has won great victories in Polynesia, but no part of the globe has witnessed fouler crimes or more atrocious wickedness on the part of white men towards savage races.

The history of the work done by members of the London Missionary Society is already a long one. As far back as 1871, the

Revs. A. W. Murray and S. McFarlane sailed from Maré, one of the Loyalty Islands, with eight native teachers, inhabitants of that group, with whom to begin the campaign against sin, superstition, and savagery in New Guinea. The first station occupied was Darnley Island, and Mr. Murray gives an incident that well illustrates the spirit in which these men, themselves trophies of missionary success, entered upon their work. Speaking about another island, the natives, in the hope of intimidating the teachers, said, "There are alligators there, and snakes, and centipedes." "Hold," said the teacher, "are there men there?" "Oh yes," was the reply, "there are men; but they are such dreadful savages that it is no use your thinking of living among them." "That will do," replied the teacher. "Wherever there are men, missionaries are bound to go." Teachers were stationed at the islands of Tauan and Sabaii. Later on, Yule Island and Redscar Bay were visited, and the missionaries returned to Lifu.

In 1872, Mr. Murray returned in the *John Williams* with thirteen additional teachers, and for the next two years superintended the mission from Cape York. In 1874, he was joined by the Revs. S. McFarlane and W. G. Lawes—who have both ever since that time laboured hard and successfully on behalf of the natives—and the steamer *Ellengowan* was placed at the service of the mission by the liberality of the late Miss Baxter, of Dundee. The native teachers experienced many vicissitudes. Some died from inability to stand the climate, some were massacred by the men they were striving to bless; but the gaps were filled up as speedily as possible, and the map recently issued (Jan. 1885) by the Directors of the Society shows that on the south-eastern coast of New Guinea, from Motumotu to East Cape, no less than *thirty-two native teachers*, some of them New Guinea converts, are now toiling in the service of the Gospel.

In 1877, the Rev. James Chalmers joined the mission, and it is hardly too much to say that his arrival formed an epoch in its history. He is wonderfully equipped for the work to which he has, under God's Providence, put his hand, and is the white man best known to all the natives along the south coast. From the first he has gone among them unarmed, and though not unfrequently in imminent peril, has been marvellously preserved. He has combined the qualities of missionary and explorer in a very high degree, and while beloved as "Tamate" (Teacher) by the natives, has added enormously to the stock of our geographical knowledge of New Guinea, and to our accurate acquaintance with the ways of thinking, the habits, superstitions, and mode of life of the various tribes of natives.

Notwithstanding various expensive expeditions for the exploration of New Guinea, he has travelled the farthest yet into the interior. He has been as far as Lat. S. 9° 2' and Long. E. 147° 42½'. The farthest point reached by Captain Armit was about Lat. S. 9° 35' and Long. E. 147° 38'. Mr. Morrison merely reached a point on the Goldie River, when he was attacked and wounded by the natives. This compelled the party to return to Port Moresby.

Mr. Chalmers is still actively engaged in his work on the great island, and he has placed many of his journals and papers at the disposal of the Religious Tract Society, in the hope that their publication may increase the general store of knowledge about New Guinea, and may also give true ideas about the natives, the kind of Christian work that is being done in their midst, and the progress in it that is being made.

The prominence which New Guinea has assumed in the public mind lately is due much more to political than to religious reasons. England is a Christian nation, and there are numbers who rejoice in New Guinea as a signal proof of the regenerating power of the Gospel of Christ. Yet, to the Christian man, it is somewhat humiliating to find how deeply the press of our country is stirred by the statement that Germany has annexed the north coast of New Guinea, while it has hardly been touched by the thrilling story of the introduction of Christianity all along the south coast. The public mind is much exercised in discussing whether Her Majesty's Government should annex the whole rather than proclaim a protectorate over a part; it hardly cares to remember the names of those who have died in trying to make known to the fierce Papuans our common brotherhood in Christ Jesus. One can understand that this is natural; still it will be an augury of good for the future of the English people, when, without losing any of their legitimate interest in public affairs, they care more for the victories won by faith alone, over ignorance, vice, and barbarism, than for the victories won by the rifle and sword, however just the cause may be in which these weapons are used.

For years past the idea has been gaining force in the public mind, both in the colonies and at home, that ultimately England would annex New Guinea. To any careful student of our history for the last century, it may appear strange that we have not done so long before. Our practice in the past has been to annex first, and to find reasons for it afterwards. To others, the very fact that even now the extremest step is only to proclaim a protectorate over a part, may appear to indicate that we are not quite so sure as we have been that annexation is wholly a blessing either to us or to the land annexed.

As already noted, in 1873, Captain Moresby did good service by accurately laying down the coastline of Eastern New Guinea. In accomplishing this, he discovered that there were several beautiful islands that had hitherto been considered part of the mainland. It is best perhaps to give what followed in his own words:—

> "The importance of our discoveries led me to consider their bearing on Imperial and Australian interests. There lay the vast island of New Guinea, dominating the shores of Northern Australia, separated at one point by only twenty miles of coral reef from British possessions, commanding the Torres Straits route, commanding the increasing pearl-shell fisheries, and also the *bêche-de-mer* fishery. It was also improved by the richness and beauty, and the number of their fine vegetable products—fine timber, the cocoanut, the sago palm, sugar-cane, maize, jute, and various vegetable fibres, fruits and rich grasses—and my conclusion, after weighing all the considerations involved, was, that it was my duty to take formal possession of our discoveries in the name of Her Majesty. Such a course secured a postponement of occupation by any Power till our Government could consider its own interests, and whilst the acquisition of these islands might commend itself, and my act result in annexation on the one hand, it might be negatived

on the other with easy simplicity, by a neglect to confirm it."

Accordingly, a cocoanut tree was transformed into a flagstaff, the British flag was run up, and duly saluted with cheers and volleys, and a picture of the proceeding adorns the captain's book as frontispiece.

Ever since that time events have tended in the direction of bringing New Guinea into closer relations with England. On the one hand, there has been the conviction that if we do not annex it some other country will, and thus threaten Australia. Then many Australians have looked upon New Guinea as a possible paradise for colonists, and have been eager to establish themselves securely upon its soil. The attempts in this direction have produced little but disaster to all concerned.

On the other hand, missionaries feel that there is much to be said on the same side. Perhaps the opinion of no one man deserves more weight than that of Mr. Chalmers. We give his views, as he expressed them before the protectorate was proclaimed.

"This question of the annexation of New Guinea is still creating a good deal of interest, and although at present the Imperial Government, through Lord Derby, has given its decision against annexation, yet the whole matter must, I have no doubt, be reconsidered, and the island be eventually annexed. It is to be hoped the country is not to become part of the Australian colonies—a labour land, and a land where loose money in the hands of a few capitalists is to enter in and make enormous fortunes, sacrificing the natives and everything else. If the Imperial Government is afraid of the expense, I think that can easily be avoided. Annex New Guinea, and save it from another power, who might harass our Australian colonies; administer it for the natives, and the whole machinery of government can be maintained by New Guinea, and allow a large overplus. We have all the experience of the Dutch in Java; I say, accept and improve.

"It will be said that, as a nation, Britain has never tried to govern commercially, or has not yet made money out of her governing; and why should she now? She does not want New Guinea. Why should she go to the expense of governing? Her colonies may be unsafe with a country of splendid harbours so near in the hands of a foreign power, and the people of that country need a strong, friendly, and just power over them, to save them from themselves and from the white man—whose gods are gold and land, and to whom the black man is a nuisance to be got rid of as soon as possible. Let Britain for these reasons annex, and from the day of annexation New Guinea will pay all her own expenses; the expenses of the first three years to be paid with compound interest at the end of that period.

"Let us begin by recognizing all native rights, and letting it be distinctly understood that we govern for the native races, not the white men, that we are determined to civilize and raise to a higher level of humanity those whom we govern, that our aim will be to do all to defend them and save them from extermination by just humanitarian laws—not the laws of the British nation—but the laws suited for them. It will not take long for the natives to learn that not only are we great and powerful, but we are just and merciful, and we seek their good.

"That established, I would suggest appointing officers in every district, whose duty it would be to govern through the native chief, and see that every native attended to plantations. A native planting tea, sugar, coffee, maize, cinchona, etc., to be allowed a bounty, and when returns arrived to be allowed so much per pound sterling. All these things to be superintended by the said officer.

"Traders would soon swarm, but no one should be allowed to trade with natives directly, but only through the Government.

"All unoccupied land to belong to the Government, and to be leased to those wishing land. No native should be allowed to part with land, and if desirous to sell, then only to the Government, who would allow him a reasonable price. Every land transaction to be made through Government; no land to be sold, only leased.

"The land revenue will be immense, and after paying all expenses, will leave much for improvements and the education of the people. Stringent laws passed directly annexation takes place to prevent importation of arms and spirits will be a true safeguard for the natives.

"As a nation, let Britain, in the zenith of her power and greatness, think kindly of the native races, and now for once in her history rule this great island for right and righteousness, in justice and mercy, and not for self and pelf in unrighteousness, blood, and falsehood. It is to be hoped that future generations of New Guinea natives will not rise up to condemn her, as the New Zealanders have done, and to claim their ancient rights with tears now unheeded. I can see along the vista of the future, truth and righteousness in Britain's hands, and the inhabitants of New Guinea yet unborn blessing her for her rule; if otherwise, God help the British meanness, for they will rise to pronounce a curse on her for ever!"

In 1883, the Queensland Government *did* formally annex their huge neighbour; but this act was subsequently repudiated by the Home Government. Towards the end of 1884, it was decided to announce a formal protectorate over a large portion of the southern shores of New Guinea.

The official ceremony took place on Nov. 6th, 1884, at Port Moresby. Five ships of war at once gave dignity to the proceeding by their presence, and astonished the natives by their salutes. About fifty chiefs were brought on board the Commodore's ship, the *Nelson*, by the Rev. W. G. Lawes. To Boevagi, the chief of the Port Moresby tribe, was entrusted the responsibility of upholding the authority and dignity of England in the island. He was presented with an ebony stick, into the top of which had been let a florin, with the Queen's head uppermost. Mr. Lawes conveyed to Boevagi the meaning of the Commodore's words when he gave the stick. "I present you with this stick, which is to be an emblem of your authority; and all the tribes who are represented by the chiefs here are to look to the holder of this stick. Boevagi, this stick represents the Queen of England, and if at any time any of the people of these tribes have any grievance or anything to say, they are, through the holder of this stick, to make it known to the Queen's officers, in order that it may be inquired into."

The formal protectorate was announced in the following terms:—

"To all to whom these presents shall come, greeting:—Whereas it has become essential for the lives and properties of the native inhabitants of New Guinea, and for the purpose of preventing the occupation of portions of that country by persons whose proceedings, unsanctioned by any lawful authority, might tend to injustice, strife, and bloodshed, and who, under the pretence of legitimate trade and intercourse, might endanger the liberties and possess themselves of the lands of such native inhabitants, that a British protectorate should be established over a certain portion of such country and the islands adjacent thereto; and whereas Her Majesty, having taken into her gracious consideration the urgent necessity of her protection to such inhabitants, has directed me to proclaim such protection in a formal manner at this place,—now I, James Elphinstone Erskine, Captain in the Royal Navy and Commodore of the Australian Station, one of Her Majesty's naval aides-de-camp, do hereby, in the name of Her Most Gracious Majesty, declare and proclaim the establishment of such protectorate over such portions of the coast and the adjacent islands as is more particularly described in the schedule hereunto annexed; and I hereby proclaim and declare that no acquisition of land, whensoever or howsoever acquired, within the limits of the protectorate hereby established will be recognized by Her Majesty;

and I do hereby, on behalf of Her Majesty, command and enjoin all persons whom it may concern to take notice of this proclamation.

"SCHEDULE.

"All that portion of the southern shores of New Guinea commencing from the boundary of that portion of the country claimed by the Government of the Netherlands on the 141st meridian of east longitude to East Cape, with all the islands adjacent thereto south of East Cape to Kosmann Island inclusive, together with the islands in the Goschen Straits.

"Given on board Her Majesty's ship *Nelson*, at the harbour of Port Moresby, on the 6th day of November, 1884."

The die has thus been cast. Already rumours that seem to have some foundation are in the air that the protectorate is soon to become annexation. It should be the aim of all to see that, by the force of public opinion, the last portion of the heathen world that has come under English protection shall have, as the years pass, many and solid reasons for thanking God that He has so guided its destinies as to unite them to our great Empire.

CHAPTER I
EARLY EXPERIENCES

Somerset—Murray Island—Darnley Island—Boera—Moresby—Trip inland—Sunday at Port Moresby—Native funeral ceremonies—Tupuselei—Round Head—Native salutations—Kerepunu—Teste Island—Hoop-iron as an article of commerce—Two teachers landed—A tabooed place—Moresby and Basilisk Islands—South Cape—House building—Difficulties with the natives—An anxious moment—Thefts—Dancing and cooking—Visit to a native village—Native shot on the Mayri—Mr. and Mrs. Chalmers in danger—Arrival of the *Ellengowan*.

Towards the close of 1877, Mr. Chalmers and Mr. McFarlane visited New Guinea for the purpose of exploring the coast, landing native teachers at suitable spots, and thus opening the way for future missionary effort. What follows is given in Mr. Chalmers's words:—

We left Sydney by the Dutch steamer *William M'Kinnon*, on September 20th, 1877, for Somerset. The sail inside the Barrier Reef is most enjoyable. The numerous islands passed, and the varied coast scenery make the voyage a very pleasant one—especially with such men as our captain and mates. On Sunday, the 30th, we reached Somerset, where we were met by the *Bertha*, with Mr. McFarlane on board of her. Mr. McFarlane was soon on board of the steamer to welcome us, and remained with us till the evening. There was very little of the Sabbath observed that day—all was bustle and confusion. Quite a number of the pearl-shelling boats were at Somerset awaiting the arrival of the steamer, and the masters of these boats were soon on and around the steamer receiving their goods.

On Tuesday, October 2nd, we left Somerset in the *Bertha*, for Murray Island, anchoring that night off Albany. On Wednesday night, we anchored off a sandbark, and on Thursday, off a miserable-looking island, called Village Island. On Friday, we came to York Island, where we went ashore and saw only four natives—one man and three boys. At eleven p.m. on Saturday, we anchored at Darnley Island. This is a fine island, and more suitable for vessels and landing goods than Murray, but supposed to be not so healthy. The island is about five hundred feet in height, in some parts thickly wooded, in others bare. It was here the natives cut off a boat's crew about thirty years ago, for which they suffered—the captain landing with part of his crew, well-armed, killing many and chasing them right round the island. They never again attempted anything of the kind. As a native of the island expressed himself on the subject:—"White fellow, he too much make fright, man he all run away, no want see white fellow gun no more." In 1871, the first teachers were landed here.

The Sunday morning was fine, and we resolved to spend a quiet forenoon on shore. We landed after breakfast, and walked through what must be in wet weather a deep swamp, to the mission house on the hill. Gucheng, the Loyalty islander, who is teacher here, looks a good determined fellow. The people seem to live not far from the mission house, so did not take long to assemble. There were about eighty at the service, including a few Australians employed by one of the white men on the island to fish for trepang. The Darnley islanders appear a much more interesting people than the Australians. Many of those present at the service were clothed. They sang very well indeed such hymns as "Come to Jesus," "Canaan, bright Canaan," which, with some others, have been translated into their language. Mr. McFarlane addressed them, through the teacher, and the people seemed to attend to what was said.

Because of a strong head wind, we could not leave the next day, so Mr. McFarlane and I returned to the shore. We found the children collected in Gucheng's house, learning to write the letters on slates. There were very few girls present—indeed, there are not many girls on the island, so many have been destroyed by their fathers at birth. We strolled about and visited the large cocoanut plantation belonging to the society. On our return we found the teacher and a number of natives collected near the beach. They had just buried a man who had died the night before—so Christian burial has begun. Formerly, the body would have been hung up and tapped, to allow the juices to run out, which would have been drunk by the friends. We returned to the mission house for dinner. I was glad to find so many boys living Gucheng. They were bright, happy little fellows, romping ab enjoying themselves.

We did not get away from Darnley Island till the morning o Wednesday, the 10th. The navigation between Darnley and Murray Islands is difficult, arising from various reefs and currents. Although only twenty-seven miles separate the two, it was Friday night before we anchored at Murray Island. We went ashore the same night.

On Saturday, we climbed to the highest point of the island, seven hundred feet high. There seems to be no lack of food, chiefly grown inland. From the long drought, the island presented in many places a parched look, and lacked that luxuriance of vegetation to which we had been so long accustomed on Rarotonga.

At the forenoon meeting on Sunday there were nearly two hundred present. Mr. McFarlane preached. A few had a little clothing on them; some seemed attentive, but the most seemed to consider the occasion a fit time for relating the week's news, or of commenting on the strangers present. The Sabbath is observed by church attendance and a cessation from work. There is not much thieving on the island; they are an indolent people. The school is well attended by old and young, and Josiah, the teacher, has quite a number of children living with him. They sing very well.

Several of the old men here wear wigs. It seems when grey hairs appear they are carefully pulled out; as time moves on they increase so fast that they would require to shave the head often, so, to cover their shame, they take to wigs, which represent them as having long, flowing, curly hair, as in youth. Wigs would not astonish the Murray islanders, as Mr. Nott's did the Tahitians after his return from England. They soon spread the news round the island that their missionary had had his head newly thatched, and looked a young man again.

On Monday, the teachers' goods and mission supplies were put on board the *Bertha*. On Tuesday afternoon, after everything was on board, a farewell service was held with the teachers, and early on Wednesday morning we left Murray Island for New Guinea. On

Friday, we made New Guinea, off Yule Island, and about sunset on October 21st we anchored about five miles off Boera. Near to the place where we anchored was a low swampy ground covered with mangrove. We could see Lealea, where there has been so much sickness. It presented the same low, swampy, unhealthy appearance. Soon after we anchored a canoe came alongside with Mr. Lawes and Piri on board. Mr. Lawes did not seem so strong as I remembered him eleven years ago, yet he looked better than I had expected to see him. He has suffered greatly from the climate. Piri is a strong, hearty fellow; the climate seems to have had little effect on him. They remained some time on board, when they went ashore in the vessel's boat—Piri taking the teachers and their wives ashore with him. The wind was ahead, and too strong for the canoe, so the men who came off in her with Mr. Lawes and Piri remained on board the *Bertha* till midnight, when the wind abated. When the boat was leaving, they shouted to Mr. Lawes to tell us not to be afraid, as they would not steal anything. They remained quietly on board till two a.m.

Mr. McFarlane and I went ashore in the morning. The country looked bare and not at all inviting. This is now the most western mission station on New Guinea proper. Piri has a very comfortable house, with a plantation near to it. The chapel, built principally by himself and wife, is small, but comfortable, and well suited for the climate. The children meet in it for school. The village has a very dirty, tumbledown appearance.

The widows of two teachers who died last year shortly after their arrival in the mission were living with Piri. We took them on board, with their things, to accompany us to the new mission. I returned ashore with the boat to fetch away the remainder of the things and teachers who were ashore, and when ready to return found the vessel too far off to fetch her, so, after pulling for some time, we up sail and away for Port Moresby. Piri and his wife came with us in their large canoe. We saw several dugongs on the way, which some esteem extra good food. Tom, one of the Loyalty Island teachers, who was in the boat with us, expressed their edible qualities thus: "You know, sir, pig, he good." "Yes, Tom, it is very good." "Ah, he no good; dugong, he much good." It must be good when a native pronounces it to be better than pork.

We arrived at Port Moresby about six o'clock. I cannot say I was much charmed with the place, it had such a burnt-up, barren appearance. Close to the village is a mangrove swamp, and the whole bay is enclosed with high hills. At the back of the mission premises, and close to them, is a large swampy place, which in wet weather is full of water. There can be no doubt about Port Moresby being a very unhealthy place. We went ashore for breakfast next day, and in the afternoon visited the school; about forty children were present—an unusually large number. Many of the children know the alphabet, and a few can spell words of two or three letters. In walking through the village in the afternoon we saw the women making their crockery pots, preparing for the men's return from the Gulf, the next north-west season, with large quantities of sago. We visited the graves of the teachers, which are kept in good order. They are all enclosed by a good fence. Within the same enclosure is one little grave that will bind New Guinea close to the hearts of Mr. and Mrs. Lawes. Over them all may be written—"For Christ's sake."

In returning from the graves, we met a man in mourning, whose wife had been killed in a canoe by natives about Round Head. He and his friends had resolved to retaliate, but through the influence of the teachers they did not do so. The teachers from the villages to the east of Port Moresby came in this afternoon, looking well and hearty. Some of them have suffered a good deal from fever and ague, but are now becoming acclimatized. The natives of the various villages are not now afraid of one another, but accompany their teachers from place to place. Men, women, and children smoke, and will do anything for tobacco. The best present you can give them is tobacco; it is the one thing for which they beg.

As it was decided that the vessel should not leave before Tuesday of the next week, Mr. McFarlane and I took a trip inland. I was anxious to see for myself if anything could be done for the natives living in the mountains. Mr. Goldie, a naturalist, with his party, was about ten miles inland. He himself had been at Port Moresby for some days, and, on hearing of our plans, he joined us, and we proceeded first to his camp. We left Port Moresby about half-past five on Thursday morning, and crossed the low ground at the back of the mission house. We ascended the hill which runs all along the coast in this district at a part about three hundred feet high, and then descended into a great plain. At present the plain is dry and hard, from the long drought, and very little of anything green is to be seen. There are a few small gum-trees, and great herds of wallabies were jumping about. The greater part of this plain is under water in the wet seasons. We walked about ten miles in an east-north-east direction, keeping the Astrolabe Range to our right, when we came to the camp, close by a large river—the Laroki. Being afraid of alligators, we preferred having water poured over us to bathing in the river.

Our party was a tolerably large one—Ruatoka (the Port Moresby teacher), some Port Moresby natives, and four Loyalty Island teachers, on their way to East Cape. We did not see a strange native all the way. We had our hammocks made fast in the bush by the river side, and rested until three p.m., when we started for another part of the river about seven miles off, in a south-east direction. Mr. Goldie also shifted his camp. After sunset we reached the point where the river was to be crossed, and there we meant to remain for the night.

We had a bath, then supper, and evening prayers; after which we slung our hammocks to the trees, in which we rested well. It was a strangely weird-looking sight, and the noises were of a strange kind— wallabies leaping past, and strange birds overhead. Mr. Goldie's Maré men joined with their countrymen, the teachers, in singing some of Sankey's hymns in English. Soon sleep came, and all seemed quiet.

At three a.m. of the 26th we struck camp, and after morning prayers we began to cross the river, which was not over four feet in the deepest part. It was here Mr. Lawes crossed when he first visited the inland tribes; so now, led by Ruatoka, we were on his track. The moon was often hidden by dark clouds, so we had some difficulty in keeping to the path. We pressed on, as we were anxious to get to a deserted village which Mr. Goldie knew to breakfast. We reached the village about six, and after we had partaken of breakfast we set off for the mountains. When we had gone about four miles the road became more uneven. Wallabies were not to be seen, and soon we were in a valley close by the river, which we followed for a long way, and then began to ascend. We climbed it under a burning sun, Ruatoka calling out, *Tepiake, tepiake, tepiake* (Friends, friends, friends). Armed natives soon appeared on the ridge, shouting, *Misi Lao, Misi Lao*. Ruatoka called back, *Misi Lao* (Mr. Lawes), and all was right—spears were put away and they came to meet us, escorting us to a sort of reception-room, where we all squatted, glad to get in the shade from the sun. We were now about 1100 feet above the sea level. We were surprised to see their houses built on the highest tree-tops they could find on the top of the ridge. One of the teachers remarked, "Queer fellows these; not only do they live on the mountain tops, but they must select the highest trees they can find for their houses." We were very soon friends; they seemed at ease, some smoking tobacco, others chewing betel-nuts. I changed my shirt, and when those near me saw my white skin they raised a shout that soon brought the others round. Bartering soon began—taro, sugar-cane, sweet yams, and water were got in exchange for tobacco, beads, and cloth.

After resting about two hours, we proceeded to the next village, five miles further along the ridge. Some of our party were too tired to accompany us; they remained where we expected to camp for the night. After walking some miles, we came unexpectedly on some natives. As soon as they saw us they rushed for their spears, and seemed determined to dispute our way. By a number of signs—touching our chins with our right hands, etc.—they understood we were not foes, so they soon became friendly. They had their faces blackened with soot, plumbago, and gum, and then sprinkled over with white; their mouths and teeth were in a terrible mess from chewing the betel-nut. On our leaving them, they shouted on to the next village. An old man lay outside on the platform of the next house we came to; he looked terribly frightened as we approached him, but as, instead of injuring him, we gave him a present, he soon rallied, and got us water to drink. By-and-by a few gathered round. We understood them to say the most of the people were away on the plains hunting for wallabies. One young woman had a net over her shoulders and covering her breasts, as a token of mourning—an improvement on their ordinary attire, which is simply a short grass petticoat—the men *nil*.

After a short stay, we returned to where we thought of camping for the night, but for want of water we went on to the village we had visited in the forenoon. We slung our hammocks in the reception room, had supper, and turned in for the night. It felt bleak and cold, and the narrowness of the ridge made us careful, even in our sleep, lest we should fall out and over. On coming across the highest peak in the afternoon, we had a magnificent view of Mount Owen Stanley, with his two peaks rising far away above the other mountains by which he is surrounded. It must have been about thirty miles off, and, I should think, impossible to reach from where we were. We were entirely surrounded by mountains: mountains north, east, south, and west—above us and below us. I question if it will ever be a country worth settling in.

We were anxious to spend the Sabbath at Port Moresby, so, leaving the most of our party, who were too tired to come with us, to rest till Monday, Mr. McFarlane, Ruatoka, and I set off on our return very early on Saturday morning, and had strangely difficult work in getting down the mountain side and along the river. Fireflies danced all round in hundreds, and we awakened many strange birds before their time, which gave forth a note or two, only to sleep again. Before daylight, we were at Mr. Goldie's camp, where we had breakfast, and hurried on for the river. We rested a short time there, and then away over plains to Port Moresby, which we reached about midday, tired indeed and very footsore. Oh, that shoemakers had only to wear the boots they send to missionaries!

Early on Sunday morning, a great many natives went out with their spears, nets, and dogs, to hunt wallabies. A goodly number attended the forenoon service, when Mr. Lawes preached. A good many strangers were present from an inland village on the Astrolabe side. There is not yet much observance of the Sabbath. Poi, one of the chief men of the place, is very friendly: he kept quite a party of his inland friends from hunting, and brought them to the services. Mr. Lawes preached again in the afternoon. As we went to church in the afternoon the hunters were returning: they had evidently had a successful day's hunting. During the day a canoe came in from Hula, laden with old cocoanuts, which were traded for pottery.

In the evening, an old sorceress died, and great was the wailing over her body. She was buried on the Monday morning, just opposite the house in which she had lived. A grave was dug two feet deep, and spread over with mats, on which the corpse was laid. Her husband lay on the body, in the grave, for some time, and, after some talking to the departed spirit, got up, and lay down by the side of the grave, covered with a mat. About midday, the grave was covered over with the earth, and friends sat on it weeping. The relatives of the dead put on mourning by blackening their bodies all over, and besmearing them with ashes.

On the 31st, the *Bertha* left for Kerepunu. As I was anxious to see all the mission stations along the coast between Port Moresby and Kerepunu, I remained, to accompany Mr. Lawes in the small schooner *Mayri*. We left on the following day, and sailed down the coast inside the reef. We arrived at Tupuselei about midday. There were two teachers here, and Mr. Lawes having decided to remove one, we got him on board, and sailed for Kaili. The villages of Tupuselei and Kaili are quite in the sea. I fear they are very unhealthy—mangroves and low swampy ground abound. The Astrolabe Range is not far from the shore we were sailing along all day. There is a fine bold coast line, with many bays.

In the early morning, our small vessel of only seven tons was crowded with natives. We left the vessel about nine a.m. for a walk inland, accompanied by a number of natives, who all went to their houses for their arms before they would leave their village. They have no faith whatever in one another. We passed through a large swamp covered with mangroves—then into a dense tropical bush, passing through an extensive grove of sago palms and good-sized mango trees. The mangoes were small—about the size of a plum—and very sweet. At some distance inland I took up a peculiar-looking seed; one of the natives, thinking I was going to eat it, very earnestly urged me to throw it away, and with signs gave me to understand that if I ate it I should swell out to an enormous size, and die.

We walked about seven miles through bush, and then began the ascent of one of the spurs of the Astrolabe. On nearing the inland village for which we were bound, the natives became somewhat afraid, and the leader stopped, and, turning to Mr. Lawes, asked him if he would indeed not kill any of the people. He was assured all was right, and then he moved on a few paces, to stop again, and re-inquire if all was right. When reassured, we all went on, not a word spoken by any one, and so in silence we entered the village. When we were observed, spears began rattling in the houses; but our party shouted, *Maino, maino* (Peace, peace), *Misi Lao, Misi Lao*. The women escaped through the trap-doors in the floors of their houses, and away down the side of the hill into the bush. We reached the chief's house, and there remained.

The people soon regained confidence, and came round us, wondering greatly at the first white men they had ever seen in their village. The women returned from their flight, and began to cook food, which, when ready, they brought to us, and of which we all heartily partook. We gave them presents, and they would not suffer us to depart till they had brought us a return present of uncooked food. They are a fine, healthy-looking people, lighter than those on the coast. Many were in deep mourning, and frightfully besmeared. There are a number of villages close by, on the various ridges. We returned by a different way, following the bed of what must be in the rainy season a large river. The banks were in many places from eight to nine feet high.

On the following morning, November 3rd, we weighed anchor and set sail, passing Kapakapa, a double village in the sea. The houses are large and well built. There are numerous villages on the hills at the back of it, and not too far away to be visited. We anchored off Round Head, which does not, as represented on the charts, rise boldly from the sea. There is a plain between two and three miles broad between the sea and the hill called Round Head. There are many villages on the hills along this part of the coast. We anchored close to the shore. A number of natives were on the beach, but could not be induced to visit us on board. We went ashore to them after dinner. They knew Mr. Lawes by name only, and became more easy when he assured them that he was really and truly *Misi Lao*. They professed friendship by calling out, *Maino, maino,* catching hold of their noses, and pointing to their stomachs. After a little time, two ventured to accompany Mr. Lawes on board, and received presents. I remained ashore astonishing others by striking matches, and showing off my arms and chest. The women were so frightened that they all kept at a respectful distance. These are the natives from an inland village that killed a Port Moresby native about the beginning of the year. When those who accompanied Mr. Lawes on board the *Mayri* returned to the shore, they were instantly surrounded by their friends, who seized the presents and made off. They had received fish, biscuit, and taro. The taro and fish were smelt all over, and carefully examined before eaten. The biscuit was wrapped up again in the paper.

On Sunday, the 4th, we were beating down through innumerable reefs, and at eight p.m. we anchored about three miles from Hula. The following morning we went up to the village, the *Mayri* anchoring close by the houses. The country about here looks fine and green, a very striking contrast to that around Port Moresby. The further east we get from Port Moresby, the finer the country looks. The people are also superior—finer-made men and women, and really pretty boys and girls—more, altogether, like our eastern South Sea Islanders. The married women spoil their looks by keeping their heads shaved. They seem fond of their children: men and women nurse them. They were busy preparing their large canoes to visit Port Moresby, on the return of the Port Moresby canoes from the west with sago.

About three in the afternoon, an old woman made her appearance at the door of the mission house, bawling out, "Well, what liars these Hula people are; some of them were inland this morning, and the chief asked them if *Misi Lao* had come, and they said no." The chief, who saw the vessel from the hill top where his village is, thought it strange the vessel should be there without *Misi Lao*, so sent this woman to learn the truth. She received a present for herself and the chief, and went away quite happy.

Next morning, November 6th, we left Hula with a fair wind, and were anchored close to Kerepunu by nine o'clock. The *Bertha* was anchored fully two miles off. Kerepunu is a magnificent place, and its people are very fine-looking. It is one large town of seven districts, with fine houses, all arranged in streets, crotons and other plants growing about, and cockatoos perching in front of nearly every house. One part of the population plant, another fish, and the planters buy the fish with their produce. Men, women, and children are all workers; they go to their plantations in the morning and return to their homes in the evening, only sick ones remaining at home; thus accounting for the number of scrofulous people we saw going about when we first landed. They have a rule, to which they strictly adhere all the year round, of working for two days and resting the third.

The *Bertha* arrived here on Friday evening. Mrs. Chalmers was at the forenoon service on the Sunday, and found there a large congregation. The service was held on the platform of one of the largest houses. Anedered preached, a number sitting on the platform, others in the house, others on the ground all round, and many at the doors of their own houses, where they could hear all that was said.

Mr. Lawes decided to remain at Kerepunu to revise for the press a small book Anedered has been preparing, and to follow us to Teste Island in the *Ellengowan*. We left Kerepunu on the morning of November 8th, the *Mayri* leaving at the same time, to sail down inside the surf. We went right out to sea, so as to beat down, had fine weather, and were off Teste Island by the 16th. After dinner we took the boat, and with the captain went in on the east side of the island through the reef, to sound and find anchorage.

When we reached the lagoon, a catamaran with three natives on it came off to us. We asked for Koitan, the chief, which at once gave them confidence in us, so that they came alongside, one getting into the boat. He expressed his friendship to us in the usual way, viz. by touching his nose and stomach, and, being very much excited, seized hold of Mr. McFarlane and rubbed noses with him, doing the same to me. He received a present of a piece of hoop-iron and some red braid, which greatly pleased him. We found the water was deep enough over the reef for the vessel, and good anchorage inside. We went on to the village, to see about the supply of water.

The people were very friendly, and crowded round us. We were led up to a platform in front of one of their large houses, and there seated and regaled with cocoanuts. The natives here are much darker than are those at Kerepunu; most of them suffer from a very offensive-looking skin disease, which causes the skin to peel off in scales. In their conversation with one another I recognized several Polynesian words. The water is obtained by digging in the sand, and is very brackish.

We came to anchor next morning, and soon were surrounded with canoes, and our deck swarmed with natives trading their curios, yams, cocoanuts, and fish for beads and hoop-iron. Many were swearing friendship, and exchanging names with us, in hopes of getting hoop-iron. There is as great a demand for hoop-iron here as for tobacco at Port Moresby. They told us they disliked fighting, but delighted in the dance, betel-nut, and sleep. The majority have jet black teeth, which they consider very beautiful, and all have their noses and ears pierced, with various sorts of nose and ear rings, chiefly made from shell, inserted. A crown piece could easily be put through the lobe of their ears.

We went ashore in the afternoon. There are three villages, all close to one another. Their houses are built on poles, and are shaped like a canoe turned bottom upwards, others like one in the water. They ornament their houses on the outside with cocoanuts and shells. The nabobs of the place had skulls on the posts of their houses, which they said belonged to the enemies they had killed and eaten. One skull was very much fractured; they told us it was done with a stone axe, and showed us how they used these weapons.

We tried to explain to them that no one was to come to the vessel the next day, as it was a sacred day. In the early morning, some canoes came off to trade, but we sent them ashore; a few more followed about breakfast-time, which were also sent ashore. In the afternoon, our old friend of the preceding day came off, with his wife and two sons. He called out that he did not wish to come on board, but that he had brought some cooked food. We accepted his present, and he remained with his family in his canoe alongside the vessel for some time, and then went quietly ashore. We had three services on board, one in the forenoon in Lifuan, in the afternoon in Rarotongan, and in the evening in English.

As Teste Island is about twenty miles from the mainland, with a dead beat to it, I decided to seek for a position more accessible to New Guinea, and as I had not a teacher to spare for this little island, Mr. McFarlane decided to leave two of the Loyalty Island teachers here. It is fertile, and appears healthy, is two and a half miles long, and half a mile broad. A ridge of hills runs right through its centre from east-north-east to west-south-west. The natives have some fine plantations on the north side, and on the south and east sides they have yam plantations to the very tops of the hills. There are plantations and fruit-trees all round the island.

On Monday, I accompanied Mr. McFarlane when he went ashore to make arrangements to land his teachers and secure a house for them. The people seemed pleased that some of our party would remain with them. Mr. McFarlane at once chose a house on a point of land a good way from our landing-place, and at the end of the most distant village. The owner was willing to give up the house until the teachers could build one for themselves, so it was at once taken and paid for. We came along to our old friend's place near the landing, when we were told that the house taken was a very bad one. In the first place, the position was unhealthy; in the second, that was the point where their enemies from Basilaki (Moresby Island) always landed when they came to fight, and the people could not protect the teachers if so far off when their foes came. All agreed in this, and a fine new house which had never been occupied was offered and taken, the same price being paid for it as for the other one. This house is close to the landing-place, and in the midst of the people. The owner of the first house offered to return the things, but we thought it would not be ruinous to let him keep them, their English value being about ten shillings.

We passed a tabooed place, or rather would have done so had we not been forced to take a circuitous path to the bush. None of the natives spoke as we passed the place, nor till we were clear of it; they made signs also to us to be silent. A woman had died there lately, and the friends were still mourning. There had been no dancing in the settlement since the death, nor would there be any for some days to come.

I think women are more respected here than they are in some other heathen lands. They seem to keep fast hold of their own possessions. A man stole an ornament belonging to his wife, and sold it for hoop-iron on board the *Bertha*. When he went ashore he was met on the beach by his spouse, who had in the meantime missed her trinket; she assailed him with tongue, stick, and stone, and demanded the hoop-iron.

The teachers were landed in the afternoon, and were well received. The natives all promised to care for them, and treat them kindly. There are about two hundred and fifty natives on the island. No *Ellengowan* appearing, we determined to leave this on Wednesday, the 21st, and to proceed to Moresby Island. Next morning we left, but, owing to light winds, we did not anchor in Hoop-Iron Bay, off Moresby Island, till the morning of the 22nd. The anchorage here is in an open roadstead. It is a very fine island—the vegetation from the water's edge right up to the mountain tops. Plantations are to be seen all round. The people live in small detached companies, and are not so pleasant and friendly-looking a people as are the Teste islanders. This is the great Basilaki, and the natives are apparently the deadly foes of all the islanders round. Before we anchored, we were surrounded by catamarans (three small logs lashed together) and canoes—spears in them all.

Mr. McFarlane decided, as soon as we came to the island, that he would not land his teachers here; and I did not consider it a suitable place as a head station for New Guinea. We left Moresby Island at six a.m. on the 23rd inst., and beat through Fortescue Straits, between Moresby and Basilisk Islands. The scenery was grand—everything looked so fresh and green, very different from the deathlike appearance of Port Moresby and vicinity. The four teachers were close behind us, in their large whale-boat, with part of their things. On getting out of the Straits, we saw East Cape; but, as there was no anchorage there, we made for Killerton Island, about ten miles from the Cape. The wind being very light, it was eight p.m. before we anchored: the boat got up an hour after us. There was apparently great excitement ashore; lights were moving about in all directions, but none came to us. In the morning, a catamaran with two boys ventured alongside of us; they got a present, and went away shouting. Soon we were surrounded with catamarans and canoes, with three or four natives in each. They had no spears with them, nor did they kill a dog on our quarter-deck, as they did on that of the *Basilisk*. They appeared quite friendly, and free from shyness. They brought their curios to barter for beads, red cloth, and the much-valued hoop-iron. The whole country looked productive and beautiful. After breakfast, we went ashore, and were led through swampy ground to see the water. On our return to the shore, we went in search of a position for the mission settlement, but could not get one far enough away from the swamp, so we took the boat and sailed a mile or two nearer the Cape, where we found an excellent position near a river. Mr. McFarlane obtained a fine new house for the teachers, in which they are to remain till they get a house built. We took all the teachers' goods ashore, which the natives helped to carry to the house. One man, who considered himself well dressed, kept near us all day. He had a pair of trousers, minus a leg: he fastened the body of the trousers round his head, and let the leg fall gracefully down his back.

On the following morning, two large canoes—twenty paddles in each—came in from somewhere about Milne Bay. They remained for some time near the shore, getting all the news they could about us from the shore-folk; then the leader amongst them stood up and caught his nose, and pointed to his stomach—we doing the same. The large canoes went ashore, and the chief came off to us in a small one. We gave him a present, which greatly pleased him. After breakfast, we went ashore to hold a service with the teachers. We met under a large tree, near their house. About six hundred natives were about us, and all round outside of the crowd were men armed with spears and clubs. Mr. McFarlane preached. When the first hymn was being sung, a number of women and children got up and ran into the bush. The service was short; at its close we sat down and sang hymns, which seemed to amuse them greatly. The painted and armed men were not at all pleasant-looking fellows.

At two in the morning (Monday), we weighed anchor and returned to Moresby Island. The wind was very light, and we had to anchor at the entrance to Fortescue Straits. Next morning, we sailed through the Straits, and, on coming out on the opposite side, we were glad to see the *Bertha* beating about there. By noon we were on board the *Bertha*, and off for South Cape, the *Mayri* going to Teste Island with a letter, telling the captain of the *Ellengowan* to follow us, and also to see if the teachers were all right.

By evening we were well up to South Cape. The captain did not care to get too near that night, and stood away till morning. About ten next morning I accompanied the captain in the boat, to sound and look for anchorage, which we found in twenty-two fathoms, near South-West Point. By half-past five that evening we anchored. The excitement ashore was great, and before the anchor was really down we were surrounded by canoes. As a people, they are small and puny, and much darker than the Eastern Polynesians. They were greatly excited over Pi's baby, a fine plump little fellow, seven months old, who, beside them, seemed a white child. Indeed, all they saw greatly astonished them. Canoes came off to us very early in the morning. About half-past seven, when we were ready to go ashore, there arose great consternation amongst the natives. Three large war canoes, with conch-shells blowing, appeared off the mainland and paddled across the Mayri Straits. Soon a large war canoe appeared near the vessel. A great many small canoes from various parts of the mainland were ordered off by those on whose side we were anchored. They had to leave. On their departure a great shout was raised by the victorious party, and in a short time all returned quietly to their bartering. It seemed that the Stacy Islanders wished to keep all the bartering to themselves. They did not wish the rest to obtain hoop-iron or any other foreign wealth. They are at feud with one party on the mainland, and I suppose in their late contests have been victorious, for they told us with great exultation that they had lately killed and eaten ten of their enemies from the mainland.

About nine, we went ashore near the anchorage. I crossed the island to the village, but did not feel satisfied as to the position. One of our guides to the village wore, as an armlet, the jawbone of a man from the mainland he had killed and eaten; others strutted about with human bones dangling from their hair, and about their necks. It is only the village Tepauri on the mainland with which they are unfriendly. We returned to the boat, and sailed along the coast. On turning a cape, we came to a pretty village, on a well-wooded point. The people were friendly, and led us to see the water, of which there is a good supply. This is the spot for which we have been in search as a station for beginning work. We can go anywhere from here, and are surrounded by villages. The mainland is not more than a gunshot across. God has led us. We made arrangements for a house for the teachers; then returned to the vessel.

In the afternoon, I landed the teachers, their wives, and part of their goods—the people helping to carry the stuff to the house. The house in which the teachers are to reside till our own is finished is the largest in the place, but they can only get the use of one end of it—the owner, who considers himself the chief man of the place, requiring the other end for himself and family. The partition between the two ends is only two feet high. Skulls, shells, and cocoanuts are hung all about the house; the skulls are those of the enemies he and his people have eaten. Inside the house, hung up on the wall, is a very large collection of human bones, bones of animals and of fish.

I selected a spot for our house on the point of land nearest the mainland. It is a large sand hill, and well wooded at the back. We have a good piece of land, with bread-fruit and other fruit trees on it, which I hope soon to have cleared and planted with food, for the benefit of the teachers who may be here awaiting their stations, as well as for the teacher for the place. The frontage is the Straits, with the mainland right opposite. There is a fine anchorage close to the house for vessels of any size.

Early next morning there was great excitement ashore. The large war canoe came off, with drums beating and men dancing. They came alongside the *Bertha*, and presented us with a small pig and food. Then the men came on board and danced. The captain gave them a return present. Mr. McFarlane and I went ashore immediately after breakfast, and found that the teachers had been kindly treated. We gave some natives a few axes, who at once set off to cut wood for the house, and before we returned to the vessel in the evening two posts were up. As the *Bertha's* time was up, and the season for the trade winds closing, everything was done to get on with the house. Mr.

McFarlane worked well. Two men from the *Bertha*, and two from the *Mayri* joined with the four teachers in the work, and by Tuesday the framework was nearly up. We landed our things that day, and immediately after breakfast on Wednesday, December 5th, we went ashore to reside; and about ten a.m. the *Bertha* left. On the Tuesday, Mr. McFarlane and I visited several villages on the mainland: three in a deep bay, which must be very unhealthy, from the many swamps and high mountains around. The people appeared friendly, and got very excited over the presents we gave them.

We got an old foretopsail from the captain, which we rigged up as a tent, in which the teachers slept, we occupying their quarters. We enjoyed a good night's rest. In early morning the house was surrounded with natives, many of whom were armed. They must wonder at our staying here: they consider our goods to consist entirely of hoop-iron, axes, knives, and arrowroot. About eleven a.m. the war canoes were launched on the opposite side of the water. The excitement here was then great. I met a lad running with painted skulls to the war canoe of the village. Soon it was decorated with skulls, shells, cocoanuts, and streamers, and launched. Those on the opposite side came out into the deep bay; ours remained stationary till the afternoon, when about thirty men got into her, and away towards Farm Bay to trade their hoop-iron for sago.

On Sunday, we met for our usual public services under a large tree, and a number of natives attended, who of course could not make out what was said, as they were conducted in Rarotongan. At our morning and evening prayers numbers are always about who seem to enjoy the singing. We see quite a number of strangers every day— some from Brumer Island, Tissot, Teste, China Straits, Catamaran Bay, Farm Bay, and other places. Those from Vakavaka—a place over by China Straits—are lighter and better-looking than those here. The women there do not seem to tattoo themselves. Here they tattoo themselves all over their faces and bodies, and make themselves look very ugly. I have not seen one large man or woman amongst them all.

We had much difficulty in getting a sufficient supply of plaited cocoanut leaves for the walls and roof of our house. By the 14th, we had the walls and roof finished, when all our party moved into it. We had a curtain of unbleached calico put up between the teachers' end and ours, and curtains for doors and windows, but were glad to get into it in that unfinished state: the weather was breaking, and we felt anxious about the teachers sleeping in the tent when it rained, and we had no privacy at all where we were, and were tired of squatting on the ground, for we could not get a chair in our part of the house; indeed, the flooring was of such a construction that the legs of a chair or table would have soon gone through it. On the 13th, we were busy getting the wood we had cut for the flooring of our house into the sea to be rafted along; got ten large pieces into the water by breakfast-time.

After breakfast, Mrs. Chalmers and I were at the new house, with the captain of the *Mayri*, when we heard a noise like quarrelling. On looking out, I saw the natives very excited, and many of them running with spears and clubs towards the house where Mrs. Chalmers, about five minutes before, had left the teachers rising from breakfast. I hastened over, and pushed my way amongst the natives till I got to the front, when, to my horror, I was right in front of a gun aimed by one of the *Mayri's* crew (who had been helping us with the house) at a young man brandishing a spear. The aim was perfect: had the gun been fired—as it would have been had I not arrived in time—the native would have been shot dead. I pushed the native aside, and ordered the gun to be put down, and turned to the natives, shouting, *Besi, besi*! (Enough, enough!). Some of them returned their spears and clubs, but others remained threatening. I spoke to our party against using firearms, and then I caught the youth who was flourishing his spear, and with difficulty got it from him. Poor fellow, he cried with rage, yet he did me no harm. I clapped him, and got him to go away. All day he sat under a tree, which we had frequently to pass, but he would have nothing to say to us. It seems a knife had been stolen, and he being the only one about the house when it was missed, was accused of taking it. One of the teachers was winding line, and he caught the young fellow by the arm to inquire about the knife. The lad thought he was going to be tied up with the line; he struggled, got free, and raised the alarm.

Only the night before I had to warn the teachers against using firearms to alarm or threaten the natives. An axe was stolen; every place about was searched for it, and for some time without its being found. At last, a native found it buried in the sand near where it was last used. It had evidently been hidden there till a favourable opportunity should occur of taking it away. During the search, the owner of the axe (one of the teachers) ran off for his gun, and came rushing over with it. I ordered him to take it back, and in the evening told them it was only in New Guinea that guns were used by missionaries. It was not so in any other mission I knew of, and if we could not live amongst the natives without arms, we had better remain at home; and if I saw arms used again by them for anything, except birds, or the like, I should have the whole of them thrown into the sea.

In the afternoon of the 14th, I went over to the house in which we had been staying, to stir up the teachers to get the things over more quickly; Mrs. Chalmers remaining at the new house to look after the things there, as, without doors or flooring, everything was exposed. I went to the seaside to call to the captain of the *Mayri* to send us the boat ashore, when, on looking towards my left, I saw twenty armed natives hurrying along. Though painted, I recognized some of them as those who were very friendly on board the *Bertha*, and spoke to them; but they hurried past, frowning and saying something I did not understand. They went straight on to the chief's house, and surrounded our party. I passed through, and stood in front of them. One very ugly-looking customer was brandishing his spear close by me. It was an anxious moment, and one in which I am sure many would have used firearms. I called out to the teachers, "Remain quiet." Our chief sprung out on to the platform in front of the house and harangued. He was very excited. Shortly he called to the teachers, in signs and words, to bring out their guns and fire. They refused. He then rushed into the house and seized a gun, and was making off with it, when one of the teachers caught hold of him. I, seeing the teacher with the chief, thought something was wrong, and went to them. We quieted him, and did our best to explain to him that we were no fighters, but men of peace. The babel all round us was terrible. By-and-by a request was made to me to give the chief from the other side a present, and get him away. I said, "No; had he come in peace, and as a chief, I would have given him a present, but I will not do so now." They retired to deliberate, and sent another request for a present. "No; no presents to men in arms. If the chief returns to-morrow unarmed, he will get a present." It seems they are vexed with our living here instead of with them, because they find those here are getting what they consider very rich by our living with them. When quiet was restored, we returned to the carrying of our things. When we came to the last few things, our chief objected to their removal until he got a farewell present. He had been paid for the use of the house before any of us entered it; but we gave him another present, and so finished the business.

Our large cross-cut saw was stolen during the hubbub. It belonged to the teachers of East Cape. It had only been lent to us, so we had to get it back. The next morning the chief from the other side came to see me. He received a present, and looked particularly sheepish when I tried to explain to him that we did not like fighting. All day I took care to show that I was very displeased at the loss of the saw, and by the evening I was told that it had been taken by those on the other side; and offers of returning it were made, but I saw I was expected to buy it from them. I said, "No; I will not buy what was stolen from me; the saw must be returned, and I will give an axe to the one who goes for it, and fetches it to me."

The following day, Sunday, the 15th, we held the usual services under a large tree near the mission house; a great many strangers present; the latter were very troublesome. On Monday afternoon the saw was returned. The *Mayri* left us that day, to visit the teachers at East Cape. The people are getting quieter. At present they are chiefly interested in the sawing of the wood for the flooring of the house. They work willingly for a piece of hoop-iron and a few beads, but cannot do much continuously. They seem to have no kind of worship, and their sports are few. The children swing, bathe, and sail small canoes. The grown-up people have their dance—a very poor sort of thing. A band of youths, with drums, stand close together, and in a most monotonous tone sing whilst they beat the drums. The

dancers dance round the men once or twice, and all stop to rest a bit.
I have been twice present when only the women danced. They bury
their dead, and place houses over the graves, which they fence round,
planting crotons, bananas, etc., inside. They do their cooking inside
their houses. It was very hot and uncomfortable when we were in the
native house. The master being a sort of chief, and having a large
household, a great deal of cooking was required. Three large fires
were generally burning in their end of the house for the greater part of
the day. The heat and smoke from these fires were not nice. Indeed,
they generally had one or two burning all night, to serve for blankets,
I suppose.

We went on with our work about the place, getting on well with
the natives and with those from other parts. We became so friendly
with the natives that I had hoped to go about with them in their
canoes. Several natives from one of the settlements invited me to visit
their place, and said if I went with them in their canoe they would
return me. I went with them, and was well received by all the people
at the settlement, where I spent some hours. On the 21st of
December, the *Mayri* returned from East Cape, and reported that all

were sick, but that the people were very friendly and kind to teachers. Anxious to keep the vessel employed, and to prepare the way for landing teachers, I resolved to visit a settlement on the mainland at deadly feud with this people. The people here tried hard to dissuade me from going, telling me that, as I stayed with them, my head would be cut off. Seeing me determined to go, they brought skulls, saying, mine would be like that, to adorn their enemies' war canoe, or hang outside the chief's house. Feeling sure that they did not wish me to go because they were afraid the hoop-iron, the knives, axes, beads, and cloth might also be distributed on the other side, I told them I must go; so they left me to my fate.

I took the teacher with me that I hoped to leave there. We were received very kindly by the people. They led us inland, to show us there was water, and when we got back to the seaside they regaled us with sugar-cane and cocoanuts. They then told us that they did not live at the village, but at the next, and merely came here for food. We then got into a canoe, and were paddled up to the other village, where a great crowd assembled, and where we publicly gave the chiefs our presents. They danced with delight, and told the teacher not to be long until he came to reside with them.

On our return we thought our friends seemed disappointed. We had suffered no harm; however, as I had been unwell for some days, and felt worse on the day following my trip, they felt comforted, and assured me it was because of our visiting Tepauri. We had several things stolen, and amongst other things a camp oven, which we miss much. Yet these are things which must be borne, and we can hope that some day their stealing propensities will change. From a very unexpected source, and in a very unexpected manner, the whole prospects of this eastern mission seemed all at once to be upset. I do not think I can do better than extract my journal for the next few days.

December 29th.—About twelve o'clock three lads from the *Mayri* came ashore to cut firewood. One of them came to me, saying, "I 'fraid, sir, our captain he too fast with natives. One big fellow he come on board, and he sit down below. Captain he tell him get up; he no get up. Captain he get sword, and he tell him, s'pose he no get up he cut head off; he get up, go ashore. I fear he no all right." They left me and went towards the sawpit. Some men were clearing at the back of my house, some were putting up a cook-house, and the teachers were sawing wood. On the cook-house being finished, I was paying the men, when, on hearing a great noise, I rose up and saw those who were at the sawpit running away and leaping the fence, and heard firing as if from the vessel. I rushed into the house with my bag, and then out to see what it was. I saw natives on board the *Mayri*, and some in canoes; they were getting the hawser ashore, and pulling up the anchor, no doubt to take the vessel. Everywhere natives were appearing, some armed, and others unarmed. Two of the lads from the vessel, wishing to get on board, went to their boat, but found the natives would not let it go. I shouted to the natives detaining it to let it go, which they did. Had I not been near, they would certainly have been fired upon by the two lads, who were armed with muskets. Before the boat got to the vessel I saw natives jump overboard, and soon the firing became brisker. I rushed along the beach, calling upon the natives to get into the bush, and to those on board to cease firing. Firing ceased, and soon I heard great wailing at the chief's house, where I was pressed to go. A man was shot through the leg and arm. On running through the village to the house, to get something for the wounded man, I was stopped to see a young man bleeding profusely, shot through the left arm, the bullet entering the chest. I got some medicine and applied it to both.

When I reached the house, I found Mrs. Chalmers the only calm person there. Natives were all around armed. When at the chief's house with medicine I was told there was still another, and he was on board. They kept shouting "Bocasi, Bocasi," the name of the man who was on board in the morning. I found a small canoe all over blood, and two natives paddled me off. On getting alongside, I saw the captain sitting on deck, looking very white, and blood all about him. I asked, "Is there still a man on board?" Answer: "Yes." "Is he shot?" "Yes." "Dead?" "Yes." He was dead, and lying below. I was afraid to remain long on board, and would not risk landing with the body; nor would it do for the body to be landed before me, as then I might be prevented from landing at all; so I got into the canoe, in which one native was sitting. The other was getting the body to place in the canoe; but I said, "Not in this one, but a larger one." So ashore I went, and hastened to the house. I understood the captain to say that they attempted to take his life, and this big man, armed with a large sugar-cane knife, was coming close up, and he shot him dead. The captain's foot was frightfully cut. He had a spear-head in his side, and several other wounds.

The principal people seemed friendly, and kept assuring us that all was right, we should not be harmed. Great was the wailing when the body was landed, and arms were up and down pretty frequently. Canoes began to crowd in from the regions around. A man who has all along been very friendly and kept close by us advised us strongly to leave during the night, as, assuredly, when the war canoes from the different parts came in, we should be murdered. Mrs. Chalmers decidedly opposed our leaving. God would protect us. The vessel was too small, and not provisioned, and to leave would be losing our position as well as endangering Teste and East Cape. We came here for Christ's work, and He would protect us.

In the dusk, one of the crew came ashore, saying that the captain was very ill, and wanted to go off to Murray Island. I could not go on board, and leave them here. We consented to the vessel's leaving, and I gave the lad some medicine for the captain, and asked him to send on shore all he could spare in the way of beads, etc. I took all that was necessary, and about half-past seven the vessel left. We were told we should have to pay something to smooth over the trouble, which we were quite willing to do. Late at night we had things ready. We had our evening prayers in Rarotongan, reading Psalm xlvi., and feeling that God was truly our refuge.

People were early about on the 30th. We gave the things which were prepared, and they were accepted. The people from the settlement to which the man belonged who was shot came to attack us, but the people here ordered them back. Many people came in from islands and mainland. A number of so-called chiefs tell us no one will injure us, and that we can go on with our work. We thought it not well to have services out of doors to-day, so held prayer-meetings in the house.

Great crowds came in from all round on the 31st, and many war canoes. The people were extremely impudent, jumping the fence, and taking no heed of what we said. One of the chief men of the settlement to which the man who was shot belongs returned from Vaare (Teste Island). He seemed friendly, and I gave him a present.

I had an invitation to attend a cannibal feast at one of the settlements. Some said it would consist of two men and a child, others of five and a child.

The people continued troublesome all day, and seemed to think we had nothing else to do than attend to their demands.

January 1st, 1878.—We were told we might be attacked. There was a great wailing assembly at the other village. A canoe from Tanosine, with a great many ugly-looking men, passed, and our friends here seemed to fear they would attack us. We thought everything settled, and that we should have no more to pay. The warp belonging to the *Mayri* was carried past to-day and offered for sale; but I would have nothing to do with it. We have tried the meek and quiet up till now, and they only become more impudent and threatening.

Having tried the peaceful and pleasant, we determined to show the natives that we were not afraid, and resisted every demand, and insisted that there should be no more leaping the fence. On demands being made, I shouted, "No more; wait, and when Beritama fighting canoe comes, then make your demands." They seemed afraid, and became less troublesome.

In the afternoon of January 2nd, the parties who have the hawser brought it to me; but I would have nothing to do with it. I told them if Pouairo, the settlement of the man who was shot, determines to attack us, let them come, we, too, can fight. One of the teachers fired off his gun at some distance from a bread-fruit tree, and the bullet went clean through a limb of it; it caused great exclamations, and crowds went to look at it.

The hawser was returned and left outside. We took no notice of it. The people were much quieter, and no demands were made. The cannibal feast was held. Some of our friends appeared with pieces of human flesh dangling from their neck and arms. The child was spared for a future time, it being considered too small. Amidst all the troubles Mrs. Chalmers was the only one who kept calm and well.

The *Ellengowan* arrived on January 20th. The natives were beginning to think no vessel would come; but when it arrived, they were frightened, and willing to forget the *Mayri* affair. A few days before she arrived some of our friends warned us against going too far away from the house. After her arrival we were able to go about among the people again.

CHAPTER II
A FEW TRIP INCIDENTS

Start eastwards from Heath Island—Naroopoo—Trading with Natives—Landing at Roux Island—Interview with the Chief—The Man with the club—Effect of a gunshot on the natives—Ellengowan Bay—Narrow Escape—The steam-whistle useful—Attempt to go inland unsuccessful—Amazons—Women chief instigators of quarrels—Toulon Island—The real "Amazons' Land"—How the report arose—Cloudy Bay—Interview with the Chief—Sandbank Bay—A hurried time—Dufaure Island—Attack on Mr. Chalmers by Aroma natives—Defended by some of the natives—Attack due to evil conduct of white men—Intentions of the natives—Heathen customs—Pigs—Planting—Trading—Sickness.

The *Ellengowan* had been thoroughly refitted at Sydney; and in the spring of 1878, accompanied by my wife, I embarked on a cruise from east to west along the south coast of New Guinea. The little steamer was commanded by Captain Dudfield, and manned by an efficient native crew. Communication was held with some two hundred villages, one hundred and five were personally visited, and ninety for the first time by a white man. Several bays, harbours, rivers, and islands were discovered and named; the country between Meikle and Orangerie Bays, together with that lying at the back of Kerepunu was explored, and the entire coast line from Keppel Point to McFarlane Harbour, traversed on foot.

In travelling through a new country, it is impossible not to have many experiences that may interest those at home, although to the traveller they may seem of little moment. In May, 1878, I began my journeys on New Guinea, in parts hereto unknown, and amongst tribes supposed to be hostile. I resolved, come what might, to travel unarmed, trusting to Him in whose work I was engaged, and feeling that no harm could come to me while in His care.

On leaving Heath Island, we really began on new and little-known seas and country, and we first anchored in a bay we called Inverary Bay. On landing, we were met by a few men, the others coming out with goods and chattels. We steamed round by the Leocadie, through what forms a good harbour for small vessels, and over by the sandbanks in Catamaran Bay. We called at Tanosina, to the east of the Leocadie, landing with caution, as these people had been rather troublesome on our first arrival at South Cape, and were very anxious to avenge the man shot on board the *Mayri*. They did not receive us heartily, and seemed inclined to be impudent, so I thought it best, after giving one or two presents, to get quietly to the boat and away. I may here say that in after-times these people were very friendly, and helped us much in our work. We visited all round the bay, returning to South Cape.

After getting a supply of water and fuel on board, we started again, going east round Rugged Head to Farm Bay, and well up to the head of the bay, anchoring opposite to Naroopoo. I landed, and soon had an admiring crowd round me. I was dressed in white, with black leather boots. Sitting on a verandah, some, more daring than others, would come up, touch my shirt and trousers, bite their fingers, and run away. Again and again this was done by the bold ones, who always eyed my boots. After consultation, one old woman mustered courage, came up, touched my trousers, and finally my boots. She was trembling all over, but horror of horrors, to add to her fear, lifting my foot, I pulled my boot off; she screamed and ran, some others setting out with her, and did not stop until quite out of sight.

After visiting several villages, and finding that the bay was thickly populated, I went on board. The following morning many canoes came alongside, and on our getting up steam were much afraid. It was evident they wanted to show us that they had confidence in us, but it was difficult with the steam up, the snorting and general commotion on board being so great. We warned them on getting up anchor to clear off. Why should they? There was no sail, nor were we going to move. A commotion aft, canoes with crews clearing away to a very safe distance. One canoe hanging on is pulled under, a wild shout, a moment's silence, and then there is a loud roar of laughter, when they see canoe and paddlers appear astern at some distance. We rounded One Tree Point and could see no entrance to a bay, just a few miles beyond, but since explored and named Lawes Bay. Keeping on, we anchored outside of the Roux Islands, in a fine safe harbour. Before leaving our friends at South Cape, they were boasting of having visited some place on the coast, where, on showing their large knives, the natives all left, they helping themselves to a good many things.

We had some difficulty in getting a canoe to come alongside, and it was not until we had fastened a piece of red cloth to a stick and floated it astern, that the first canoe would come near. The natives approached, picked up the red cloth, and in showing them pieces of hoop-iron, they gradually came near enough to take hold of a piece, look well at it, and finally decide to come alongside. Once alongside we were soon fraternizing, and on seeing this other canoes came off, and trading for curios began. Asking the captain to keep on trading as long as possible, I hastened ashore, to see the chief of one of the villages. As long as trading canoes remain alongside, the parties landing are perfectly safe; care should be taken to get away as soon as possible after the canoes leave the vessel.

The tide was far out when our boat touched the beach. A crowd met us, and in every hand was a club or spear. I went on to the bow, to spring ashore, but was warned not to land. I told them I had come to see the chief, had a present for him, and must see him.

"Give us your present, and we will give it to him, but you must not land."

"I am Tamate, from Suau, and have come as a friend to visit your old chief, and I must land."

An elderly woman came close up to the boat, saying, "You must not land, but I will take the present, or," pointing to a young man close by, "he will take it for his father," he being the chief's son.

"No; I must see the chief for myself; but the son I should also like to know, and will give him a present too."

Springing ashore, followed by the mate, a fine, daring fellow, much accustomed to roughing it on the diggings, and not the least afraid of natives, I walked up the long beach to the village, to the chief's house. The old man was seated on the platform in front of the house, and did not even deign to rise to receive us. I told him who I was, and the object of my coming. He heard me through, and treated the whole as stale news. I placed my present on the platform in front of him, and waited for some word of satisfaction; but none escaped the stern old chieftain. Presents of beads were handed to little children in arms, but indignantly returned. Loud laughing in the outskirts of crowd and little jostling.

"Gould," said I to the mate, "I think we had better get away from here; keep eyes all round, and let us make quietly to the beach."

To the chief I said, "Friend, I am going; you stay." Lifting his eyebrows, he said, "Go."

We were followed by the crowd, one man with a large round club walking behind me, and uncomfortably near. Had I that club in my hand, I should feel a little more comfortable. When on the beach we saw the canoes had left the vessel, and were hurrying ashore; our boat was soon afloat, still, we had some distance to go. I must have that club, or I fear that club will have me. I had a large piece of hoop-iron, such as is highly prized by the natives, in my satchel; taking it, I wheeled quickly round, presented it to the savage, whose eyes were dazzled as with a bar of gold. With my left hand I caught the club, and before he became conscious of what was done I was heading the procession, armed as a savage, and a good deal more comfortable. We got safely away.

From Fyfe Bay we went round to Meikle Bay, where I visited all the villages, and was well received. Before landing I decided to walk inland, and see for myself if there was no arm of the sea running up at the back. The charts showed no such thing, but I felt sure, from the formation of the land and the manner of clouds hanging over it, that there must be a lake or some large sheet of water, and that there must be considerable streams carrying off the water of the Lorne Range and Cloudy Mountains, as no stream of any size came to the sea on the coast-side. I got the chief of the village at the head of the bay and a large following to show us the way. We travelled for some miles through good country, and at last came out opposite a large sheet of water, stretching well up towards Cloudy Mountain and away towards the head of Milne Bay. Seeing the Stirling Range, I was able to take a few positions.

Our mate, who had his fowling-piece with him, saw a very pretty parrot on a cocoanut tree. He approached until close under—the natives, about forty in number, standing breathlessly round, and wondering what was going to happen. Bang! Down dropped the parrot; a wail, hands to ears, a shout, and we were left alone with the chief, who happened to be standing close by me. Those natives only ceased running when they reached their homes.

We visited several villages, and at sundown returned. In the dark we travelled along the bed of a creek, passing small villages, whose inhabitants were terribly alarmed, but none more so than our chief. Poor fellow, he *was* frightened. How nimbly he ascended his platform on our arrival at his house, where his two wives were crying, but now rejoiced to see him in the body. Long ago the escort had returned with a terrible tale, and they feared whether their husband could have lived through it all. But he was now considered a veritable hero, to be sung in song and shouted in dance. Friends gather round; he tells his tale; presents the bird; the wives examine it, then the crowd of relatives. He afraid! oh dear no! But he looked pale for a native, and no quantity of hoop-iron would induce him to move from that platform and the side of those dear wives that night. Enough for one day, one month, one year, so, "Good-bye, Tamate; I shall be off in the morning to see you." Arriving on board late, we were welcome: they feared we had been spirited away.

The following day we got round to Ellengowan Bay. After visiting all the villages, I went right up to the head of the bay to see Silo and its chief. The tide was very low, and after pulling the boat some distance through mud we left her in charge of the two rowers, the mate and I going to the village. He had hoop-iron cut in seven-inch lengths in his pockets. The old chief received us graciously, and began giving me a long story of what he wished to do in the way of pigs and food, if I would only stay two days. It was a sickly looking hole, and not being quite rid of fever, I hoped to get on board and away in an hour. A large crowd gathered round, all under arms, very noisy, and certainly not gentle. A slight scuffle took place, but was soon over. The mate missed some of his hoop-iron, caught one young man with a piece, and took it from him. The crowd increased. I told the chief I should prefer his people unarmed, and not so noisy. He spoke to them, some put down their clubs and spears; but they were hidden in the bush close by. We bade the chief good-bye, but he expressed a great wish to see me in the boat. Apparently with great carelessness, we made towards the beach, attended by a noisy crowd, all arms now picked up. Remembering the difficulty we had in landing, and knowing savages preferred killing out of their own villages, hospitality having ended when friends left the precincts, I determined not to have that crowd near the boat. I asked the chief to send them back; but to him they would not listen, and still the noisy crowd followed on. I shouted to them to return, and not come troubling us, as we were getting into the boat. No use; on they followed, and the boat they meant to visit. I stood still, and not feeling particularly cheerful, I told them to go on, and go off to the vessel—that I should wait and return to the village. Stamping my foot, as if in a towering passion, I told the chief, "Go with all your people to the boat; as for me, I shall return." It had the desired effect. The people fled, and the few who remained listened to the old man, and came no further. We got to the boat and away, glad to escape without any unpleasantness.

Entering Orangerie Bay, we anchored off the village of Daunai, from which the whole district takes its name. When here, our Chinese cook lost his knife, and, spotting the thief, determined to have it; but our captain prevented him from jumping into one of the canoes, and so avoided trouble. There were over one hundred canoes round the vessel, and altogether over four hundred men.

We stopped all trading, and frightened the canoes away by blowing the steam whistle—they were much afraid of it, and kept at a very respectful distance.

We went up the long sheet of water we saw when we crossed Meikle Bay, finding it in every way suited to its native name, Paroai, or piggish water, and quite useless as a harbour for anything larger than an ordinary boat. I went ashore in one of the canoes, to be landed at Bootu, and walk across to Milne Bay. Before leaving the vessel I engaged with the natives to take me right away to the head of the lagoon, and when I had seen Milne Bay, to return me to the vessel, when they would be paid for all their trouble. So with our bags and a few eatables, we started; when about a mile away from the vessel, they headed the canoe more in towards the right shore, and no amount of talk in calmness or wrath would get them to do otherwise. We touched at a place not far from a village we visited overland—some left us, and we were certainly now too weak to proceed. We ran down to the village, where we landed with my bag, and away went my native canoe men. Love or money would not move the villagers, and they were exceedingly impudent, knowing well that we were quite in their hands. My friend the mate, who insisted on accompanying me, agreed with me that things were rather out of the common with us, and that a sharp eye, and quick ear, and quick action were of some importance. They at once went to get their clubs and spears, and begged and insisted on presents; but they were astonished, I doubt not, to find their begging of little avail.

"Go to the vessel, if you want presents."

"Why are you anchored so far off?"

"Can't get nearer, and only wish you would show me the way in close to here."

Pointing to a passage close in shore, I suggested they had better take us off, and we would try and get her round when the tide rose; but to this they objected, and instead of becoming more friendly, it seemed to us they were just going the other way; but that may have been merely as we thought, looking at them through coloured glasses, suspicion, and a certain mixture of doubt if ever we should again see the vessel. A few men came running along the beach. I met them, and hurriedly asked them to take us off when they would have hoop-iron and beads.

"Yes."

"Quick! do not let them think! Into the nearest canoe."

Away in the distance those in the village were shouting and gesticulating.

"Come back! Come back, at once."

"Oh no, my friends; pull, you must pull!" and while they are discussing we are paddling. I tell them it would be dangerous to attempt going back. On we go, beyond small islands in sight of vessel, and now they give up speaking of returning. We got off, and I paid the fellows well. Anxious to get in, we tried in many places at high tide to enter the shore channel, but all was useless. For several miles we were sailing deep in mud, unable to work the engine. A canoe came near, and I told them to inform those ashore that we could not get in.

At Port Glasgow, the people cleared out, bag and baggage, leaving us in quiet possession. At Port Moresby, I had heard of a woman's land, a land where only women—perfect Amazons—lived and ruled. These ladies were reported to be excellent tillers of the soil, splendid canoeists in sailing or paddling, and quite able to hold their own against attacks of the sterner sex, who sometimes tried to invade their country. At the East End they knew nothing of this woman's land, and nowhere east of Hula have I ever heard it spoken of.

To find so interesting a community was of great moment, and everywhere we went we inquired, but only to be laughed at by the natives; sometimes asked by them, "How do they continue to exist?" But that, too, puzzled us. As no part of the coast from East Cape to Port Moresby would be left unvisited by us, we were certain to come across the Amazonian settlement, and when we did, it would be useful to keep a sharp look-out, as I have noticed that the instigators of nearly all quarrels are the women. I have seen at South Cape, when the men were inclined to remain quiet, the women rush out, and, as if filled with devils, incite them. Just after the attack on the *Mayri*, and when I was going about the settlement attending to the wounded, I heard the women call loudly for vengeance, and, because the men would not at once heed them, throw their shields on the ground and batter them with stones, then pull their hair, and tell the men they were only poor weak cowards.

We heard that Mailiukolo (Toulon) canoes with women were more numerous, and some very large ones with women alone. In the early morning we were off the island, and soon ready to land. On crossing the reef we met two canoes, one with men and one with women. We signed to them to go to the vessel, whilst we pulled up to the large village on the north side. As the boat touched the fine hard sandy beach, a man, the only being in sight, ran down and stood in front. I went forward to spring ashore, but he said I must not. Finding he knew the Daunai dialect, I said to him, I must land; that I was a friend, and gave him my name, which he already knew from the east. I gave him a strip of red cloth and stepped ashore, when he ran away into the bush. At our first approach I could only see this one man, but now I saw hundreds of grass petticoats on women standing under the houses. I could not see the upper parts of their bodies, only the petticoats and feet. They were indeed quiet until I advanced nearer, when one wild scream was given that would try stronger nerves than mine, and signs to keep away. It required more inquisitiveness than I possessed to proceed. I retired a few paces, warning the boat's crew to keep a good look-out, and especially from the bush end of the village, where the man ran to. I invited the dusky damsels to come to me, if they objected to my visiting them; but no, I must return whence I came; they had seen me, that was enough.

"No, my friends; we must meet, and you will have some presents."

I held up beads and red cloth, but, strange to say, they seemed to have no effect on that curious crowd. I never saw so many women together. How were we to meet? was now the question; to be baulked by them would never do. I threw on the beach a piece of red cloth and a few beads; walked away quite carelessly, and apparently not noticing what was taking place. A girl steals out from the crowd, stops, turns, eyes fixed on me; advances, stops, crosses her hands, pressing her breast. Poor thing! not courage enough; so, lightning speed, back. It is evident the old ladies object to the younger ones attempting, and they are themselves too frightened. Another young damsel about nine or ten years old comes out, runs, halts, walks cat-like, lest the touch of her feet on the sand should waken me from my reverie; another halt, holds her chest, lest the spirit should take its flight or the pattering heart jump right out. I fear it was beyond the slight patter then, and had reached the stentorian thump of serious times. On; a rush; well done! She picks cloth and beads up.

I have gained my point, and will soon have the crowds—no need to wait so long to have the baits picked up now, and, after a few more such temptings, it is done. I am besieged by the noisest crowd I have ever met, and am truly glad to escape on board the boat. We went to the vessel, and brought her round to the west side, where we anchored, and I again landed. Crowds met me on the beach, but no men. I gave my beads indiscriminately, and soon there was a quarrel between the old ladies and young ones. The latter were ordered off, and, because they would not go, I must go. The old ladies insisted on my getting into the boat, and, being now assisted by the few men we met in the canoe, I thought it better to comply. Long after we left the beach we heard those old cracked, crabbed voices anathematizing the younger members of that community. I suppose I was the first white mortal to land on that sacred shore, and I must have been to them a strange object indeed.

I am fully convinced that this is the Woman's Land, and can easily account for its being called so by stray canoes from the westward.

After leaving the island, we steamed round to the westward of the small islands in Amazon Bay, where we intended to spend a quiet Sabbath after a hard week's work, and previous to beginning another. After anchoring, canoes with men and boys kept crossing from the mainland, and all day Sunday it was the same. They halted at the islands, and with the next tide went on to Toulon. Landing on the Saturday evening to shoot pigeons, we met several natives, and learned that their plantations were on the mainland, and that they crossed to plant and fight, taking their boys with them. Afterwards at Aroma, they told me they left their wives and daughters at home in charge of a few men, whilst the majority crossed to the main, and stayed away for some time, returning with food, to spend a few days at home on the island. During their absence, the women sail about and trade, going as far as Dedele in Cloudy Bay, being one and the same people. Canoes from the westward might have called at Toulon when the men were on the mainland fighting and planting, and seeing only women, would soon report a woman's land. Many years ago an Elema canoe was carried away there. They were kindly treated by the Amazons, but at Dedele on returning, were attacked and several killed; they naturally reported a woman's land too.

The following week we visited Dedele in Cloudy Bay, which had been visited two years previously by Messrs. Lawes and McFarlane. The village was barricaded with high and thick mangrove sticks, with a narrow opening to the sea. They objected to my landing, and formed a crescent in front of the boat. I sprung ashore and asked for the chief. I held out a piece of hoop-iron, and a rather short, well-built man, dressed with boar's tusks and other ornaments, stepped forward and took my present. He took me by the hand, and led me to the village, just allowing me to peep in at the opening. I could see the women rushing out by an opening at the other side; pigs, dogs, nets, and other valuables were being carried off; they were rushing off wildly away into the bush. I was very anxious to get right in, and meant to before I went to the boat. My beads were all done up in small parcels, so I could throw them about easily. A poor old woman was sitting under the nearest house, bewailing her sad lot, with an infant, the mother of which had very likely gone off to the bush to hide the valuables and to return for the child, or perhaps she was upstairs packing up. I threw the poor old dame a packet of beads for herself and another for the child. Spying another old lady close by on the opposite side, I threw her one. It had the desired effect; my friend, the chief, who stood guard at the opening, now conceived the "happy thought" that something could be made out of me.

"Would you like to walk round and look at the village?"

"Yes, I should."

"Come, then;" and, giving me his hand, he led me, attended by an armed crowd, to every house, on the verandahs of which I deposited a packet of beads. He was the chief, and was named Gidage. When going round he said—

"You are no longer Tamate, you are Gidage."

"Right, my friend; you are no longer Gidage, you are Tamate."

I gave him an extra present, and he gave me a return one, saying, "Gidage, we are friends; stay, and I, Tamate, will kill you a pig."

"No, Tamate. Gidage must go; but hopes to re-return, and will then eat Tamate's pig."

"No, stay now; we are friends, and you must be fed!"

"No, I cannot stay; but when I return, then pig-eating"—not a very pleasant employment when, other things can be had.

Pigs are very valuable animals here, and much thought of, and only true friends can be regaled with them. The women nurse the pig. I have seen a woman suckling a child at one breast and a small pig at the other; that was at South Cape. I have seen it also at Hula and Aroma. Proceeding to the beach, we parted, old and well-known friends.

"Gidage, must you go?"

"Yes; I cannot now stay, Tamate."

"Go, Gidage; how many moons until you return?"

"Tamate, I cannot say; but hope to return."

"*Kaione* (good-bye), Tamate."

"*Kaione*, Gidage;" and away he started, leaving Tamate on the beach, surrounded by an interesting crowd of natives.

It was near here, a few years after, that a *bêche-de-mer* party of seven were murdered; and on the opposite side of the bay two cedar-seekers were waylaid, and lost their lives. We went into Sandbank Bay, and I landed at the village of Domara. What a scene it was! The women rushed into the long grass, and I was led, after a good deal of talk, up to the village—only to see, at the other end, grass petticoats disappearing, the wearers hidden by the quantity of stuff they were carrying. One poor woman, heavily laden with treasures, had perched above all her child, and away she, too, was flying. Never had white man landed there before, and who knows what he may be up to?

The following incident illustrates the shocks a traveller must put up with in New Guinea.

It was resting-day at a village, far away from the coast, and, spreading my chart out on the middle of the floor in the small native house in which we were camping, several sitting round, I was tracing our journey done, and the probable one to do, when strange drops were falling around, a few on the chart. They came from a bulky parcel overhead. Jumping up quickly, I discovered that they were grandmother's remains being dried. Our chart was placed on the fire, and the owner was called lustily, who hurriedly entered and walked away with the parcel. It was altogether a hurried time, and spoiled our dinner. Feeling convinced that a suitable locality for the settlement of teachers might be found in the neighbourhood of Orangerie Bay, I resolved on returning thither, and we anchored at Kuragori, on the east side of Dufaure Island, on April 25th, 1879. I went ashore, and found the people delighted to meet me. The chief, Tutuaunei, seems a fine young fellow. The people are good-looking, clear-skinned, and very few suffering from skin disease. They were quite at home with us, and a number accompanied me inland. In strong trade winds, the vessel could lie under the lee of the mainland opposite. We got on board, and steamed round to the north side, anchoring off Bonabona.

I went ashore, and was met on the beach by Meaudi, the chief. He is the chief of four villages, some distance from one another, and all a good size. I visited all four. They have good houses, and all looks clean. I saw no mangroves whatever, and no appearance of swamp. The villages are on the beach, and I believe in good healthy positions. We walked from Bonabona to Sigokoiro, followed by a large number of men, women, and children, who were much interested in my boots, clothes, and hat. The chief lives in Gokora, and when on the platform in front of his fine large house I gave the present, and we exchanged names. By adopting his name, it meant I was to visit all his very special friends, and give them also presents. I called an old woman sitting by to come to me. Very hesitatingly she came, and stretched forth her arm to receive a present. I asked her to come nearer, which she did, when assured by the chief it was all right, and I put her present of beads round her neck. Then all the people shouted, clapped their hands, and danced with delight. After that, all the old women were produced. We were well known by report to them, and so Tamate passed as a great *taubada* (chief).

Dufaure is a fine island, quite equal to any I have seen in the South Pacific—plantations on all sides, right up to the mountain tops. They know nothing of firearms, for, on inquiring if there were birds on the island, they asked if I had a sling. The people are a much finer race, and freer than any I have seen further east. The two races seem to meet here—that from the Kerepunu side, and that from the east. We are anchored some distance from the shore in three fathoms, and further out it is shallower. The opposite shore on mainland looks low and unhealthy.

There are ten villages on the island, five of which we have visited.

After visiting the Keakaro and Aroma districts, our journeyings were nearly brought to a sudden termination. When we got halfway between the point next to McFarlane Harbour, and Mailu, where there is a boat entrance, we saw the boat, and waved to them to approach. They came near to the surf, but not near enough for us to get on board. The native of Hula, from Maopa, got on board. The Hula boy got on board early in the day, leaving us to go on alone. I called out to them to proceed to the boat entrance at Mailu. Great numbers of natives were with us; we saw, in the distance, numbers more sitting on the beach, and armed. Some of those following us were armed. When within two miles of where the boat was to await us, we came upon a crowd of men and women; the former carried spears, clubs, or pieces of hard wood, used in opening cocoa nuts; the women had clubs. Some time before this, I said to the teacher and Loyalty islander, "Keep a good look-out; I fear there is mischief here." When we came upon the last group, I asked for a cocoanut in exchange for beads; the man was giving it to me, when a young man stepped forward and sent him back. We hastened our steps, so as to get to the village, where the strangers from Mailukolo and Kapumari might help us. The teacher heard them discussing as to the best place for the attack; and, not knowing that he knew what they said, he heard much that left no doubt in our minds that murder was meant. I carried a satchel, which had beads and hoop-iron in it; they tried to get it. I gave presents of beads; some were indignantly returned. I was in front, between two men with clubs, who kept telling me I was a bad man. I held their hands, and kept them so that they could not use their clubs. The Loyalty islander had a fowling-piece—thinking we might be away some days, and we might have to shoot our dinners. They tried hard to get him to fire it off, and twice tried to wrest it from him. They know what guns are, and with reason. They tried to trip us; they jostled us. On we went.

Two men, when near the village, came close up behind me with large wooden clubs, which were taken from them by two women, who ran off to the village. Things looked black, and each of us prayed in silence to Him who rules over the heathen. Soon a man came rushing along, seized the club, and took it from the man on my left, and threw it in the sea. He tried to do the same with the one on my right; but he was too light a man, and did not succeed. An old woman, when at the point, came out and asked them what they meant, and followed us, talking to them all the way, so dividing their thoughts. An old chief, whom we saw on our way up, came hurriedly along to meet us, calling out, "Mine is the peace! What have these foreigners done that you want to kill them?" He closed up to the teacher, and took him by the hand. Another chief walked close behind me. They began to talk loudly amongst themselves. Some were finding fault that we should have been allowed to get near the village, and others that there was yet time. The boat was anchored some distance off: we got her nearer; and, when ready to move off to the boat, I opened my satchel, gave hoop-iron to our friends the chiefs, and threw beads amongst the crowd. I shouted for Kapumari, and a sturdy young fellow fought his way through the crowd. I gave him a piece of hoop-iron, and, with our friendly chiefs, he forced the crowd back, calling on us to be quick, and follow. So into the water we got, the chiefs calling, "Go quick; go quick!" We got on board; our Chinamen got flustered, and very nearly let the boat drift broadside on the beach; we, with poles and oars, got her round and off, sails set, and away for Kerepunu. Before changing clothes, we thanked God our Father for His protection and care over us. We felt He alone did all; unsettled their thoughts as to who first, where, and when; and it was He who gave us friends.

Why should they want to kill us? It was surely never for the small satchel I carried. I believe it was revenge. Some years ago, a vessel called off Aroma; trading for food was done on board; thieving went on; food was sold twice; revolvers and rifles were brought out; the natives were fired on, several were wounded, and very likely some were killed. Natives on the beach were fired upon, and some were wounded who were hiding in the bush close by. We land—the first foreigners to visit them—and on us they will be revenged. What a pity that the same foreigners who fire on the natives do not return the following week, and so receive their deserts! The wretches steer clear of such parts. I have asked the teacher to find out, if possible, why Aroma wished to kill Tamate and Taria.

When in the boat, we asked the Hula boy why he left us and took to the boat. He said he had heard some say we should be killed, and that we would make a fine feast. He did not tell us, because he had not an opportunity, and was afraid the people might hear him if he told, and so he would be killed.

A week later a chief from Maopa came with a Kerepunu chief to see me. I recognised him as the one who kept back the crowd the other day at Aroma, and opened the way for me to get into the water, and so into the boat. He says, from our landing in the morning they had determined to kill us, but the suitable time did not arrive. When we arrived at the place where the large canoes from Toulon and Daunai were lying, it was there arranged by the Aroma people and those from the canoes that Aroma should kill us and have all they could get, and those from the canoes should have the bodies to eat. He says they kept putting it off, until, finally, it was to be done when we were at the boat, then they would have boat and all; but he and two other chiefs arrived just in time. He says it was not revenge, and, turning to the Kerepunu chief, he said, "You know Aroma from of old, and how all strangers are killed." I gave him a present, and told him that I hoped to see him soon.

The inhabitants of the inland villages are probably the aborigines, who have been driven back to the hills by the robuster race now occupying their plantations on the coast. Their habits and customs are curious and interesting. They cook the heads of their slain enemies, to secure clean skulls to put on sacred places.

They have one great spirit—Palaku Bara, who dwells in the mountains. They worship him unitedly in one place. Each family has a sacred place, where they carry offerings to the spirits of deceased ancestors, whom they terribly fear. Sickness in the family, death, famine, scarcity of fish, etc.—these terrible spirits are at work and must be propitiated.

Pigs are never killed but in the one place, and then they are offered to the spirit. The blood is poured out there, and the carcase is then carried back to the village, to be divided, cooked, and eaten.

Pigs' skulls are kept and hung up in the house. Food for a feast, such as at house-building, is placed near the post where the skulls hang, and a prayer is said. When the centre-post is put up, the spirits have wallaby, fish, and bananas presented to them, and they are besought to keep that house always full of food, and that it may not fall when the wind is strong. The great spirit causes food to grow, and to him presentations of food are made.

Spirits, when they leave the body, take a canoe, cross the lagoon, and depart to the mountains, where they remain in perfect bliss; no work, and nothing to trouble them, with plenty of betel-nuts. They dance all night long, and rest all day. When the natives begin planting, they first take a bunch of bananas and sugar-cane, and go to the centre of the plantation, and call over the names of the dead belonging to their family, adding, "There is your food, your bananas and sugar-cane; let our food grow well, and let it be plentiful. If it does not grow well and plentiful, you all will be full of shame, and so shall we."

When they go on trading expeditions, they present their food to the spirits at the centre post of the house, and ask the spirits to go before them and prepare the people, so that the trading may be prosperous.

No great work and no expedition is undertaken without offerings and prayer.

When sickness is in the family, a pig is brought to the sacred place of the great spirit, and killed. The carcase is then taken to the sacred place of the family, and the spirits are asked to accept it. Sins are confessed, such as bananas that are taken, or cocoanuts, and none have been presented, and leave not given to eat them. "There is a pig; accept, and remove the sickness." Death follows, and the day of burial arrives. The friends all stand round the open grave, and the chief's sister or cousin calls out in a loud voice, "You have been angry with us for the bananas we have taken (or cocoanuts, as the case may be), and you have, in your anger, taken this child. Now let it suffice, and bury your anger." The body is then placed in the grave, and covered over with earth.

CHAPTER III
SKETCHES OF PAPUAN LIFE

Journey inland from Port Moresby—Evening with a chief—Savage life—Tree houses—Uakinumu—Inland natives—Native habits of eating—Mountain scenery—Upland natives—Return to Uakinumu—Drinking out of a bamboo—Native conversation—Keninumu—Munikahila—Native spiritists—Habits and influence of these men—Meroka—Kerianumu—Makapili—The Laroki Falls—Epakari—Return to Port Moresby.

In 1879, I made a long journey inland, in a north-easterly direction from Port Moresby. I visited many native villages, and explored the mountainous country along the course of and between the Goldie and Laroki rivers.

The reader will get some notion of the country, the natives, and their customs, from the following extracts taken from a journal kept at that time.

July 15*th*, 1879.—We left Port Moresby at half-past seven, reaching the Laroki at half-past eleven. We crossed in shallow water near to where the Goldie joins the Laroki. We had eighteen carriers, four of them women, who carried more than the men. After resting awhile at the Laroki we went on about three miles farther to Moumiri, the first village of the Koiari tribe of Port Moresby. On entering the village we took them by surprise; the women shouted and the men rushed to their spears. We called out, *Mai, mai, mai* (Peace, peace, peace), and, on recognizing who we were, they came running towards us with both hands outspread. We met the chief's wife, and she led us up the hill, where there are a number of good native houses. It was shouted on before us that foreigners and Ruatoka had arrived, and down the hill the youths came rushing, shaking hands, shouting, and slapping themselves. We were received by the chief under the house, and there we had to sit for a very long time until his wife returned from the plantation with sugar-cane. Our carriers chewed large quantities of sugar-cane, got a few betel-nuts, and then set off on the return journey. We are now thirteen miles north-east from Port Moresby, 360 feet above sea-level, the thermometer 84° in shade. The people are small, women not good-looking, and children ill-shaped. The Goldie runs at the base of the hill; the natives get water from it. The houses are very similar to those inland from Kerepunu. On the door hangs a bunch of nutshells, so that when the door is shut or opened they make a noise. Should the occupants of the house be asleep, and their foes come, they would, on the door being opened, be woke up. Spears and clubs are all handy.

16*th*.—Ruatoka, Joe (an African), and I started at half-past ten for Munikahila, where we hope to get carriers, our Moumiri friends objecting to go. The first village we came to we found deserted, and in one old house the skeleton of a child. We crossed to another village, and coming suddenly upon the few who were at home, they were terribly frightened; one woman danced up and down the village, and shouted to the people in the neighbouring villages to come at once. We are 1170 feet above sea-level, at a village called Keninuma. The people soon gathered round, some with spears, clubs, and shields, others unarmed. Feeling cold after the climb, I signed to be allowed to go into a house to change clothing, and was given to understand that a very good place to do it was on the verandah in front of the house, and before the assembly. When the chief, Poroko Butoa, arrived, we were assigned a small house; a man during the evening came rushing along with one piece of sugar-cane and calling out for a tomahawk. A tomahawk for a piece of sugar-cane would be throwing money to the winds. We are E.N.E. from Moumiri.

17*th*.—Rather cold during the night. Five natives who slept in the house with us kept a fire burning all night. A child sitting in front of the house has a taro in one hand, a bamboo pipe in the other; takes a bite of the taro, then a draw from the charged pipe, and the mixture seems to be thoroughly relished. Feeling sure we should get carriers here, we took no supplies with us, so are now eating the best we can get, doing Banting to perfection. A number of men have been sitting all day about the house making spears, the jawbone and tusks of the wild boar being the only implements.

18th.—Thermometer at sunrise 70°. A number of ugly painted and feathered fellows came in this morning on their way to the village in the valley. The people here are much darker than the coast tribes, and their hair is woolly. Joe said on arriving here, "Hallo, these people same as mine, hair just the same." They are scarcely so dark. A few are bright-coloured, but all have the woolly hair. A goodly number suffer from sores on feet and other parts of body. Their one want is a tomahawk. The people seem to live in families. We had a good supper of taro and cockatoo, the latter rather tough.

19th.—The carriers have not yet arrived. In the evening a woman shouted and yelled; all rushed to their spears, and there was great running, snorting, and blowing at some imaginary enemy. After the chief came in, we lay about the fire for some time; then to our blankets. I was beginning to nod, when some women in a neighbouring house began giggling and laughing. Our friend wakened up and began talking. I told him to sleep; he answered, *Kuku mahuta*, (Smoke, then sleep). He had his smoke, and then began reciting. I remember, as a youth, being told, when I could not sleep, to repeat a psalm or paraphrase, or count one hundred to myself, and I should soon drop off. This fellow repeated aloud and he must have been going over the mythologic lore of his family for very many generations, and yet he did not sleep. At last, a smoke, beginning with a scream of *kuku*. Now, surely sleep; but no, he changed to a low monotonous chant, so grating on the sleepy man's nervous system that it would have driven many desperate. At last, in the morning hours, the notes became indistinct, long pauses were observed, and, finally, I fell asleep.

The women carry exceedingly heavy loads up these steep hills. Yesterday one woman had two large kits of taro, and a child of about two years on the top of all. Ruatoka shot eight blue pigeons and one bird of paradise to-day: the latter must be eaten with the best of all sauces—hunger. The natives pick up heads, legs, and entrails, turn them on the fire and eat them.

20th.—Yesterday evening, about six, the carriers came in with great shouting, and glad was I to see my lad and companion Maka then. Great was the joy at the division of salt and tobacco. Before we came here the women and children slept in the bush at night, the men in the village. They are at enmity with the natives on the flat across the ravine, and it seems that sometimes they get a night visit, and may lose a man. For the last two nights the women have been in the village, but every sound heard causes a shout. Last night, when just getting off, they came rushing up to our house, and calling on us to get up with our guns, as their enemies were coming. "Only fire off one, and it will frighten them away." We told them to go and sleep, and not be afraid.

The state of fear of one another in which the savage lives is truly pitiful; to him every stranger seeks his life, and so does every other savage. The falling of a dry leaf at night, the tread of a pig, or the passage of a bird all rouse him, and he trembles with fear.

How they relish salt! The smallest grain is picked carefully up. Fortunately we have a good deal of that commodity. Never have I seen salt-eating like this; only children eating sugar corresponds to it.

Here as in all other parts of New Guinea—it is not the most powerful man who fights and kills most, but little abominable sneaks, treacherous in the extreme. Since our arrival here we find the thermometer from 82° to 84° during the day, and as low as 68°, more frequently 70°, during the night. By bearings we are only about twenty miles in straight course from Port Moresby.

21*st*.—The village is built on the ridge, the chief's house right on the high end and looking east, our small house close by on the side of the others, on each side, leaving a pathway in the centre. At the very end of the ridge is a house on a very high tree, used as a look-out house and a refuge for women and children in case of attack. There are quite a number of tree houses in the various villages on the ridges seen from here. The people are anxious to get Maka, a light-coloured and very fine-looking native lad, married to one of their girls and settled down amongst them. I said to our African, "They want Maka to marry one of their girls." Joe, I suppose, felt slighted that he too had not an offer, and he replied, "Well, sir, in Madagascar, a very big chief was real anxious I marry his daughter; fine-looking girl; he make me chief, and give me plenty land; far cleaner people than them be."

I find the people have the same sign of friendship as in the east end of New Guinea—nose and stomach pointed to. They speak of a land, Daui, with which they are friendly, a very long way off. Daunai, of Orangerie Bay, is called Daui in some places. To their tree houses they have ladders with long vines on each side to assist ascent. Our delay here will help us to know the people. I have just been showing them the likenesses of two young friends, and the excitement has been great, men, women, and children crowding round, thumb in mouth, scratching and shaking heads, and leaping and screaming, coming again and again to have a look.

22*nd.*—A number of strangers slept, or rather made a noise all night in houses close by, and amongst them a spiritist, whose hideous singing and chanting of revelations was enough to drive one frantic. We tried to quiet him, but it was of no use—silenced he would not be. A man sitting by us when having morning tea asked for some of the salt we were using. We told him it was not salt, but sugar. He insisted it was salt, and we gave him some on his taro. He began eating, and the look of disgust on his face was worth seeing; he rose up, went out, spat out what he had in his mouth, and threw the remainder away.

23*rd.*—Cannot get the natives to move; they say they are tired, and will have to rest until to-morrow morning, and they are also afraid of their enemies. The excitement is great, but what it all means is difficult for us to say. Noon: all have cleared out with spears, clubs, and shields, two men having been killed in a village near, and they have gone to get hold of the murderers if they can. Dressed in their feathers and fighting gear, with faces streaked, they do certainly look ugly. After being some time gone, they returned, saying the enemy, who were from Eikiri, had gone off to the back mountains.

28th.—Left this morning, and had to carry our things, no natives accompanying us. When about four miles on, we met natives who willingly took our bags and accompanied us to Uakinumu. The travelling was not so bad—a good deal of descending and ascending. Oriope, the old chief, was delighted to see us. His wives and children have gone with great burdens of betel-nuts and taro to trade at the seaside. The old fellow goes with us. We are now 1530 feet above sea-level, east-by-south from last camp—Mount Owen Stanley due north. Oriope is Mr. Lawes's great friend. He used to live in Munikahila, but trouble through marrying a wife has sent him in here. He seems greatly attached to Ruatoka. He is a terrible talker, long-winded and deafening.

29th.—We had a strange sort of a hut for sleeping-quarters on the top of a rock. The house, being open all round, felt exceedingly cold when the fire went down. The people here seem much lighter than at the other place, and the children have a more pleasant expression. Basaltic rocks lie scattered about in every direction. We had our flag flying, and the admiration was great, the natives viewing it from underneath then from a distance, and in each position noticing something new. About half-past eleven we left. The old chief and four carriers went with us. After crossing the head of the Munikahila Creek we passed through fine thickly-wooded country, that may yet become a very extensive coffee country. After travelling for some hours, we camped 1800 feet above sea-level. On the way the carriers struck and were for going back, but we insisted on their going on a little further. Strange formation of country all around here. This ridge seems alone in a large basin, one side of which is bare perpendicular rock. There is a good quantity of cedar, but so difficult to get away that it would never pay to work. We are north-east from Uakinumu.

30th.—We started late, continued our journey along the ridge, rising gradually to 2250 feet, and then along a fine level country for some miles, when we began to descend. Soon our old friend began shouting, and received an answer from a village a long way off. Close by us was a very steep descent, down which we went till we came under the shadow of a great rock, where we rested, and in about an hour up came ten natives unarmed, touched our chins, and we theirs, then all squatted to smoke. One of them, some time ago, had been to the coast, and knew Rua; his joy at now seeing him in here was great. A shot had been fired at a cockatoo before they heard the shouting, and they were much afraid. When all seemed satisfied, and the crust of the news broken, I proposed a start, so up bundles, and away we went. When having gone about two miles, there was a halt in an open space, and we were given to understand we must camp there. I could not agree to it, "We must go on to the village." "No, you must stay here."

"We cannot; we must go on."

"If you go on you will be devoured by the *boroma badababa* (great pig)."

I insisted upon going on; they called to those in the village, and on being answered we again went on for about half a mile, when every bundle was put down and a halt called, and again we had to listen to the unintelligible story of the wild animal or animals that would destroy us. We sat down and tried to get them to see as we did, that a house was necessary for our comfort. A thunderstorm was working up, and soon the rain would be down on us—let us be off for the village. They had a long confab with those in the village on the ridge, which, when ended, seemed favourable; and so up the steep side of the ridge we went. When halfway up they halted, and wanted us to camp under the shelter of a great rock. Seeing some young men with bundles rounding the rock, I joined myself to them, and away we went, followed by the others to the village. Under the first house in the village sat a man, with a large pig standing by him, which he was clapping and scratching, as if to keep it quiet; and as we went along we saw great pigs under the houses. Certainly they were savage-looking pigs. We were given an open house, and the rain was coming on. I was ascending, when it became necessary to spring from a pig that was after me. Is this Goldie's big beast the natives told him of? This is a fine country. We passed through large plantations of yams, taro, sugar-cane, and bananas. During the evening we had crowds of men and lads—no women or children—to see us. Some are quite light copper-coloured, others are very dark; nearly all are dressed with cassowary feathers; many with ruffs round their necks made from these feathers. There were none very tall, but all seem well-built men, with good muscle. They have the same calabashes and chunam sticks for betel-chewing as at Kerepunu. Some chunam sticks made from cassowary bones are well carved. They are a very noisy lot; one would think they were trying to see who could speak the loudest. They tell us it is impossible to cross to the other side, as further inland the ridge ends—and there is nothing but bare broken rook—inaccessible all round. The majority of the men are bearded and moustached, and have cassowary feathers like a pad behind, on which they sit. They dress with a string. The demand for salt is very great; grains are picked up, and friends are supplied with a few grains from what they have got for taro. The name of the place is Kenagagara, 1810 feet above the sea-level, E.N.E. from Uakinumu.

31st.—Great crowds of people keep going and coming. We spent a miserable night. Our old chief, Oriope, had a conclave round the fire, and it took him all night to recount the doings of the Naos (foreigners), not forgetting the toilet. At times he waxed eloquent, and the whole gully rung again. It was useless telling him to be quiet. All men and lads have the nose and ears pierced. A number of women and children are about. Some of the women are fine, tall, muscular, and clear-skinned, as light-coloured as Eastern Polynesians. The children are lithe, blithe, and hearty—some very dark and some very light. The women have brought large quantities of taro for salt. Oriope is very sleepy, and I have every now and again to wake him up, so that to-night he may sleep soundly, and not prevent our sleeping.

My name here is Oieva—that of the fine-looking old father of the village. At present I am all alone the others being out after birds. The natives are very friendly. They relish salt and ginger, which I have tried with them, and which they pronounce good. Ruatoka and Maka have returned; they shot a pig, which the natives who accompanied them cooked and divided, to be carried in. The excitement is great over the division, and the whole assembly are shouting; those from the hunt recounting the day's proceedings, acting the shooting of the pig, to the intense delight and amazement of the others. They eat flesh nearly raw. A pig is put on the fire until the hair is well singed off; then division is made, then re-divided, and eaten. They take a piece between the teeth, hold with one hand, and with a bamboo knife cut close to the mouth. A bird is turned on the fire a few times, then cut up and eaten.

August 1*st.*—Left this morning to look for a track. We passed through a fine large village about one mile from here, and were joined by sixty men, all armed with spears and clubs, and faces painted. They accompanied us for about four miles, and then turned away to the south. We continued on the ridge for some miles further, until we could see that all round were great inaccessible mountains with bare faces. It begins with the Astrolabe, extending west until Vetura is reached, and then away east by south until the centre of the range is reached. In some places it has a perpendicular rock face of many hundred feet; in other places it is broken rock with bush growth, and only at very long distances can tracks be found, and even then it is difficult to get up. We descended to the river, a large one, flowing west, through great rocks, often lost, sometimes only pools appearing here and there until, some distance down, and when eight hundred feet above sea-level, it comes out a fine and flowing river. We had a good bath, and, of course, the inevitable *kuku*, and then skirted the side of the ridge, passing close by and under great rocks and overhanging cliffs, and up a most extraordinary steep path into splendid sugar-cane and taro plantations. Weary, we sat down and ate sugar-cane under the shade of a great rock. This West Indian "long breakfast" goes well when thirsty and hungry. The natives who accompanied us, having caught a large rat and frog, turned them on the fire and ate them.

A truly wonderful country! What terrible convulsions of nature there must have been here ere these great boulders were displaced and rolled about like mere pebbles! The villages are so built that they are accessible only on two sides by very narrow tracks. We saw no game of any kind, yet the cassowary must abound somewhere near, as every one of the natives wears great head-dresses and neck-ruffs made from the feathers. Our highest ascent to-day was to 2360 feet above the sea-level; we call it Mount Bellamy; it stands out alone, and from it we saw the Astrolabe, Vetura, and Munikahila.

2nd.—We left this morning for a pig and cassowary hunt, but were unsuccessful. We bagged four cockatoos, one green parrot, one brueros, and three pigeons. Of my travelling in this land, to-day beats all; it was along mere goat tracks, on the edge of frightful precipices, down precipitous mountain-sides and up steep ridges, on hands and knees at times, hanging on to roots and vines, and glad when a tree offered a little rest and support. I gave it up at last, hungry and weary, and let the others proceed. I stayed with a party of natives who were getting a kind of large almond with a very thick fleshy rind, the nut inside very hard, which they broke open with stones, filling their kits with the kernels. They call the nut *okari*. They fed me with sugar-cane, taro, and *okari*, and then got leaves for me to rest on. They had all their arms handy; I was, as I am always, unarmed, and felt thoroughly comfortable with them. Only once in New Guinea have I carried a weapon, and then we had spears thrown at us. I consider a man safer without than with arms. The return "home" was frightfully steep and trying to wearied and hungry folks.

3rd.—Youths busy with feathers of cockatoos got yesterday, making head-dresses. They take the feather, strip it down, throw the quill away, fasten all the stripped feathers neatly together, dry in sun, then bind round their combs. One youth is preparing a head-covering from the bark of the mulberry: he is making native cloth by chewing the bark, and no wonder he complains of his jaws being sore, for it is a long job. I gave the children presents of beads this morning, and some of the old gentlemen objected, saying they ought to have had them; but I did not understand them. It is very convenient at times not to understand what is said—it is thoroughly native. We have been asking them if they will receive teachers, and they all say yes, and at once, for it means tomahawks, knives, and salt. They say, "To-morrow we'll all go and get the two teachers at Munikahila and bring them here now." We here are in excellent health and spirits; a little disappointed at not being able to cross. Certainly we have not lived on the best, and we have camped anywhere. I like these mountaineers—free, independent, and kind. When they cook taro, if near, we get a hot taro to eat, and often they bring hot taro to the house. They bring their presents of taro and sugar-cane and at once walk away. They have very good houses, thatched with grass, some with a verandah on two sides, and all built six feet and more from the ground. When we were away yesterday, a wild boar from the bush took possession of the village. Often when the natives are in the bush they have to seek refuge in climbing trees from the savage tuskers, especially if they have been speared, and are determined to fight. Our flag is flying, to signify that it is "resting day."

The natives very seldom bury their dead, leaving the body in a house set apart for it, which they often visit. When a number of deaths take place, they leave the village and settle somewhere else not far off. There is one grave here, near to our house, on which a tobacco plant is growing, a bamboo pipe, the property of the deceased, alongside, and a few sticks on end with yams on top. When they do bury, the body is placed standing in the grave.

4th.—We left Kenakagara this morning, accompanied by natives. Our friends soon left us, and we lost our way, and after some hours' travelling found ourselves in a thick bush and surrounded by precipices. It has been up hill and down dale with a vengeance, trying hard to get to the south-west. At last, wet through and thoroughly tired, we camped to have breakfast, dinner, and supper in one. We were ten hours on the tramp, and carrying our bags, so feel ready for a night's rest.

5th.—We see where we are; but how to get out is the problem to be solved. Ruatoka has gone to look for a track. We had a fine night, a roaring fire at our feet, and so enjoyed sleep. Camping this way is preferable to living in native huts, far more comfortable and enjoyable; but for our work it is better for us to be with the natives. Uakinumu bears south-west-by-west from us now, and could be reached in a few hours, if only we could get down the precipice. Rua has returned. When some distance off, he heard cooeying, and responded, when our old friend, who had been looking for us in a great state of fear, shouted his name. Rua told him to follow, and he did so, arriving at the camp soon after. He was so excited he could not speak, but embraced us all round, and then sat down.

After breakfast, we set off, each carrying a bundle. The travelling was difficult, until we arrived on the path leading to the creek and up to Uakinumu. When on the spur, the old man shouted for the youths to come and help us; they cooeyed back, and we hoped to see them in about an hour, or at the most two hours; after waiting and no one coming, we descended, and when at the creek met a youth coming slowly along and saying others were following. I felt sure they delayed their coming to meet us until we should be near the village, where they would take the bags and receive tobacco and salt; but they were sold; we trudged on, and would not let them have a bag. We took no notice of those we met, and to their solicitations asking to carry bags we turned a deaf ear. The chief's eldest son came along and begged to have my bag. No, on no condition. The poor old chief was in a sad state; but as we are likely to require their services some future day, it is necessary to teach them that for work or service they will be paid, but for skulking, and hoping to get tobacco and salt, their hopes are futile. We reached the village, and Oriope did all he possibly could to keep us. No, on we will go; his sleepy boys may sleep on. We gave him and his little grandchild who accompanied him presents, bade him good-bye, and away.

6th.—Here, and in all the villages we have been, we have seen very few women and girls, and very few of the young men seem to be married. Do they kill the girls when born?

7th.—Left this morning for a mountain close by, hoping to see the windings of the Laroki from it. We had to descend 1000 feet, and then ascend 1800. From the droppings about, I should say the cassowary and pig abound in the gullies about this mountain. We found on the top a deserted village and five cocoanut-trees. We could make nothing of the Laroki, because of thick bush on top. We saw that the Munikahila creek flows west and south, until, due north of this, it turns sharp and flows north-by-east and falls into the Goldie. We reached camp with thoroughly whetted appetites, and enjoyed breakfast and dinner of pigeons and taro. We call the mountain Mount Elsie. It is north of Vetura, and west and south of Keninumu. We have seen four new villages close to one another where a teacher could work well. We have now five positions for teachers, and I hope before we have finished with this inland trip to have thirty, giving four and five villages to each teacher. In crossing one of the spurs, a native and his son brought us bananas, and water in a bamboo. It is difficult to drink out of a bamboo. Place the open end to the mouth, raise gradually, look out, here it comes—steady. Ah, too much raised; it is a deluge streaming over you and nearly choking you. Try again— well, a little better, yet far from perfect. Choking, are you? Never mind, practise, and you will soon be an expert—a native in drinking, truly. The natives have been having a feast. They began with boiled bananas and finished with a large snake cooked in pots. It was cut up and divided out amongst all—sixteen eggs were found in her, a little larger than a good-sized fowl's egg. They seemed to relish it much, and the gravy was much thought of. They say pig is nothing compared to snake. Ah, well, tastes differ.

9th.—We had a few noisy strangers in the village, and they seemed to be anxious that all they had to say should be heard in every house. The conversation is kept up by the inmates of the various houses, and at times all are speaking and trying to drown one another. A lull comes, and you fancy the turmoil is ended, and so roll on your side for a sleep; but, alas, it was only drawing breath, the noise being perhaps worse than before. Our chief and his wife had a quarrel over something or other last evening. Of course the woman had the best of it. Strange, she said very little, but that little seemed to be to the point. Every now and again he would shout, *Pirikava! pirikava! pirikava!* (Dear me! dear me! dear me!), and then scream and rage. The wife would then laugh at him, which made him worse, screaming and dancing more than ever. She would then say something, which he would answer, and so quieted him down a little. All have gone hunting to-day—men, women, and children, pigs and dogs. Before leaving, they told us if we saw any one sneaking about, we were to be sure to shoot them; but if they came up openly to us, and pointed to the nose and stomach, they were friends, and had come for salt and tobacco. We get our water in canvas bags, and teachers or missionaries coming inland will require a set of water-bags made from the very best canvas.

11*th*.—A number of natives have gone to Port Moresby, to help Rua and Maka with tomahawks, salt, &c. After they left, we went to the bush, and cut down a number of trees for posts for a house. The chief, Poroko, has given us land, at an elevation of 1260 feet; splendid view all round; and if not healthy, I know not where to go, unless it be to the top of Mount Owen Stanley. There will be plenty of room for taro, sugar-cane, and coffee plantations. A woman often passes us with a frightful load of taro and sugar-cane on her back, and on the top of all an infant in a net basket. She goes to the next house, swings the infant kit off first, placing it on the ground, where the infant in it kicks and rolls, but cannot get cut until the kits of taro and sugar-cane are safely housed.

14*th*.—This morning, after an early breakfast, we started with the Port Moresby natives for Munikahila, they being anxious to secure a supply of betel-nuts to return with. Have promised our old friend Oriope of Uakinumu, before we started on the Eikiri trip, that if he led us across and gave us bearers, all should have tomahawks, knives, etc. He did not carry out his part, and the bearers from him returned, leaving us inland. I was anxious to pay them for what they did, so we went on there with tomahawks, tobacco, and salt. We were about two miles from the village, when we shouted, and were replied to, and soon four young fellows came rushing along, in a great state of perspiration and very excited, rubbing our chins and throwing their arms around us, highly delighted that we had returned. They were not going to serve us as they did the last time. We reached the village, and were seated with strangers and surrounded by old friends, when Oriope, who had been on his plantation, came along to where we were, nearly breathless, and streaming with perspiration; he threw his arms around me, embraced me, rubbing his dirty moist cheeks on mine, sitting down and not speaking for some time. When he began, he said he was afraid we were terribly offended, and would not return; but, having returned to him, we must stay. No, we cannot; we must return to Keninumu that night. Ah, he could manage it; he would have us tied, and so detain us. Four coast natives who knew the Koiari language were with us. We told our old friend we wanted a large quantity of betel-nuts, and that he had better set out at once for them. Soon the women and lads were off. We then removed to our old house on the rock, and there told him, through the interpreter, what we had expected of him, and that he had not done it, but that having told him we should pay them, we had come now to do so for the journey made. We gave our tomahawks, tobacco, and salt, and the old man was truly delighted, saying, "I and my people will take you wherever we may go with safety." He does not go to sea on the other side, as Mr. Lawes supposed, and says it is impossible to cross over unless we go up by Yule Island, and there he says it is dangerous, because of the cannibals. In returning, I saw, for the first time in New Guinea, a bush of the real South Sea Island *kava* (*Piper methysticum*).

17*th.*—We have just had a service, and through Kena we have told the natives the object of our coming and staying, that they might know of the true God, and of Jesus Christ the Saviour. It was interesting to mark the different expressions on their faces as they heard for the first time of God—the God of love, and that as His servants we were here. When told of the resurrection they looked at one another; some laughed, others seemed serious. They were very particular in their inquiries as to the name of the Great Spirit, and of His Son—forgetting, and returning to hear it again.

18*th.*—Here we are at Uakinumu for another trip; but alas, alas! cannot get carriers. The young men are all off wallaby-hunting, so we must start. This evening, a woman came in with several bamboos of grubs, which were cooked in the bamboos, then spread on leaves; some salt was dissolved in the mouth and squirted over all, and it was amusing to see the gusto with which men, women, and children partook. Oriope is very persistent in wanting a teacher. He was greatly delighted when I gave him a large knife; he examined it all over, then pressed it with tender affection to his bosom. Fearing lest some friends who are with him at present might ask it from him, he returned it to me, requesting me to keep it until they left.

20*th.*—Last night, after turning in, I heard a peculiar noise, as of some one in great distress, then loud speaking in a falsetto voice, and knew then what was up—we had a spiritist in the village, and revelations were now about to be made. We were all named, and the places we were to visit. I felt somewhat anxious as to the revelation, for if it should be the least doubtful as to our going, no native would stir with us. However, the revelation, on being interpreted to us by Kena, was all right; we were good men, and kind, and the villages would all willingly receive us. The spirit dilated at length on the good qualities of foreign tobacco and the badness of the native stuff, and wound up by asking for some foreign. Oriope at once got up and gave from his own stock what was wanted. These native spiritists are terrible nuisances; they get whatever they ask, and the natives believing so thoroughly in them, they have the power of upsetting all arrangements and causing serious trouble. This morning, I found our spirit friend to be a man who sat in our house all day yesterday, a stranger from an inland village. He has quite a different look from the other natives—an anxious, melancholy expression. While at morning coffee, he came and sat down alongside of us all right, and we learned from him that the spirit of a deceased friend comes into him, and then things are revealed, the spirit speaking through him. He says, when we were at Eikiri, a few weeks ago, he knew it, and told the people of his village of it.

The wallaby-hunters are to come in this afternoon with great supplies. When sitting round the fire with our old chief, we asked him if he knew of any tailed folks about inland. "Oh dear, yes." And then he gave us a perfect and laughable description of what must be some creature of the monkey tribe. It climbs, laughs, and talks a peculiar language of its own; it scratches the head, slaps the thigh, and sits down to eat like a man. I then said, "But they are not really men?" "Well, not exactly, but very near it; they are hairy all over, and some are perfectly black." The tail, according to his description, must be about a fathom long. We are to see them, and must, he says, secure one or two, dead or alive. Our spirit is out in his prognostications, the wallaby-hunters have not returned, and we cannot leave to-morrow.

21st.—Our spirit friend is quite out as yet, for here we are nursing Patience, and trying to make her a dear friend. We are promised a start to-morrow. In the evening, the hunters came in with large supplies of wallaby. They report innumerable horses and foreigners as having gone to Kupele; we suppose it to be Goldie's party. From to-day's shooting, the old man got a green parrot, and devoured it raw. Oriope dressed himself in his fighting gear, and went through a few antics; he looked a perfect fiend. He is very proud of a stone club he possesses with a piece broken off; he says it was broken in felling a tremendous fellow in a neighbouring village. He killed him. "What, stand before me!"

22nd.—I was eating a banana this morning, when I was told not to throw the skin away, but hand it to them, which I did, when it was passed round and kissed by all with short ejaculations. I asked what it meant, and was told it was their manner of thanking the spirits for ripe bananas. We started at eight a.m. with eight carriers and our old friend, and twenty inland natives returning home with wallaby; one poor woman had two large kits on her back, and an infant in another, hanging in front of her. We were seven hours on the tramp, along a good path, on which horses could get along well. The most difficult ascent was shortly after we left Uakinumu; but the path was good. The last hour of travelling was in a thunderstorm, with a regular tropical pour of rain. When we neared the village Marivaeanumu, the men came rushing out with their spears and shields, thinking it was an attacking party; but on seeing Maka, who was just behind the first native, and I following up, they shouted out, *Nao, nao!* (foreigners), and ran back with their spears. The village is small, and the houses very dilapidated; it is 1800 feet above sea-level. Maka was buying taro with salt, and having finished, some natives noticed damp salt adhering to his hand; they seized the hand, and in turn licked it until quite clean. Grains of salt falling were sought for and picked up. The shields here are the same as at Hood Bay, beautifully made. They are going to fight soon with another district, and are making great preparations in spears, clubs, and shields.

23rd.—Our spiritist gave us a very short and indistinct séance last night. A man speared the other day in a wallaby hunt, near the Laroki, he told us, was dead. He seemed to be raving a great deal, and wound up the first part with, *Nao kuku daure* (Foreign tobacco is bad). Continuing to rave and disturb sleep, I told Oriope that, if that spirit did not at once go back where it came from, I should certainly have to make it; he reported what I said, and the spirit thought it advisable to leave. We started this morning after a good breakfast, and had good travelling across a fine level country E.S.E. for about four hours, crossing several times the head of the Laroki: it is a magnificent country for horses. In somewhat thick scrub, a youth met the first of our party, and was fraternizing very feelingly with them: I appeared, and he took to his heels, and no calling of friends or foreigners could bring him back. We came suddenly upon a woman and two children, and, poor things! they went into a terrible state; nothing would comfort them; beads, tobacco, and salt lost their charm on them. The family pig was with them; it danced, grunted, advanced, retired, and finally made at me. In the morning I took a piece of plaster from my heel, and threw it into the fireplace; instant search was made for it by about a dozen natives; it was found, and handed back to me, they making signs that I should throw it somewhere else. Yesterday morning I unthinkingly put the loose hair from my comb into the fire, and great was the outcry.

We are now in Nameanumu, in the Sogeri district, and in a fine house twelve feet from the ground. We are about 1530 feet above sea-level. Teachers here need have no difficulty about food; there is a great abundance all round of taro, banana, sugar-cane, and bread-fruit. A teacher with some "go" in him, and a good earnest wife to help him, would do well here. I am inclined to think an easier way here will be from Moumiri; but we have to travel with natives where they can take us with safety to themselves. Sitting round the fire a little while ago, our spirit friend having just left us, an old woman shouted out to Oriope to look out, as the spirit was about to go through the thatch near to where he was sitting. Instant search was made, but nothing found. She then called out from her verandah that it had gone, as Rua and Maka were doing something with their guns. I may say the old woman was with us last night, and heard my threat. We have had the description here of some other animal that is in the Kupele and Moroka districts. It is a dangerous one to go near, and several have lost their lives from it.

24th.—Very heavy rain. A number of people have come in from the villages to have a look at us, so I have to go through the process of baring arms and chest. This forenoon they described an animal to us that I think must be the tiger—a long animal, with a long tail and large paws, treads lightly when seeing its prey, and then bounds upon it, tearing the bowels out first. They say they are as long as the house—twelve feet. We are not prepared to tackle such, customers. Our host is a quiet man, with a very pleasing expression of countenance. I like the people much, and pray God the day is near when they shall have the Gospel preached unto them, and receive it, and know it to be the power of God unto salvation. Evil spirits reign over them, and the utterance of every rascally spiritist is thoroughly believed.

They seem very much attached to their children, and in their own peculiar way, I dare say, love their wives. Husband and wife meeting after a separation is strange. Some who returned with us had been away for a fortnight; their wives looked pleased when they saw them, so did the husbands; not a word was spoken, only a look; clubs and spears were put down, and the husbands went to where other men were sitting, the wives to light fires and cook food; when cooked, the wife took it to the husband, who ate a little, gave away some, and then went and sat by his wife. I have noticed that the wives are particularly happy when preparing this return food. Oriope's wife, who accompanied us, is ill with a cold; I wished her to take a dose of chlorodyne, but she cried and hesitated much; the old man then took the cup and told her to look; he drank some of it, said it was not bad, and then pressed her to drink it off, which she did.

25*th.*—We left this morning at eight, and arrived at Orofedabe, in the Favele district, at one p.m. The walking was good and steady, the first few miles along the valley beneath a mountain in the Sogeri district, which we called Mount Nisbet, and the range near to Eikiri. We crossed the Laroki several times, and sat near its head; then ascended an easy ridge of the Owen Stanley Range. We travelled for about two hours along this ridge, then descended, crossing two streams, which we suppose to be the head streams of the Kemp Welch, flowing into Hood Bay. There are six small villages on ridges close by, high mountains all round, and not far off the mountain on which the wild animal lives. They tried to persuade us that this was Meroka, and there was no use our going further; but we could not believe it, and I brought my compass out, and pointed to them where Eikiri,

Sogeri, Kupele, and Hapele were, and told them where I expected to find Meroka, which cannot be very far off. When they saw I knew something of our position, they said we could not get to Meroka, because of rocks and wild beasts. At the village we slept the last two nights they did all they could to detain us, because of the salt and beads. They were assisted by Oriope, who was anxious that all should go to his cousin and friends, with whom we were staying. In a conversation they had under the house, shortly after we arrived, I could hear sufficient to enable me to understand they would keep us there, and not let other villages get salt and beads. I got thoroughly vexed with the old man, and told him he could return home, and that unless we saw numerous villages with plenty of people we should not again return here. He turned right round, and told us we should see Favele and Meroka, and many villages, only we must return to his cousin's; that was all right, we certainly should return. This morning, I told him to remain and take care of his wife; that the people here would lead us and carry our things. He begged of me to leave some of the things to ensure our return, and I did so. Some of the people here are very dark and others very light.

26th.—They tried hard to prevent our going to Meroka this morning, saying we should be eaten by the *Jakoni* (wild beast)—and how could they return? That would not do—go I must; so I got the things out, and asked some Meroka natives, who had come in, to pick them up and let us start. They refused, and joined in with our friends, saying we had better remain. No; I must see Meroka, and until I saw it not a taro would be bought nor a pile of salt given. They all sat down, looking true savages. After some time, I said, "Meroka, or we return at once." I got my bag and went on to the path; they got up, and called to me to come back—they would go to Meroka, but leave the things, and return here to sleep. No; I must have the things; I might want to sleep at Meroka. That was terrible, the salt would be finished, and there would be none for them here. Would I not consent to their taro being bought, and then they would go with me? No; Meroka first, and taro when we return.

Seeing there was nothing for it—that go I would—they consented, and the Meroka folks picked up the things, and away we went. It was a short walk across the side of a ridge, down about 600 feet and up to 1500, and then along another ridge. We soon had crowds to see us, men, women, and children; and all were delighted, for we bought their taro. The village we stayed at was new, and they told us formerly they lived further in on the mountain, but a man was eaten by the *Jakoni*, and they came down. A number of natives were in mourning for the man eaten. After some time, we got up to ascend the ridge, to have a good view of the villages and decide on our position. They tried hard to prevent us, but we went on, a few following to the next village. They pretended great fear of the *Jakoni*, and at some places begged of us to tread lightly, and not to speak. It was all a ruse to get us back. We went on, and up to the highest village, where we had a splendid view. We counted fourteen villages on the ridges in the Meroka basin and on the other side of the river we had crossed, and as many more known as Havele. I believe it would be much easier to get here from Eikiri than from Sogeri. The natives of Oriramamo, the highest village, told us they went from there to Eikiri in one day.

The people of Meroka are very mixed, some very dark, others very light. Some of the women had quite an Eastern Polynesian look; some of the children were well-formed, and really pretty. A few men had light-coloured whiskers; curly heads abounded, although a number had straight hair. They say they are not Koiari. The Koiari comprises Munikahila, Eikiri, Sogeri, Taburi, Makapili Pakari; and Eikiri is N.W. from Oriramamo; Mount Bellamy is W.N.W. A high round mountain, I have named Ben Cruachan, east; Mount Nisbet, W.S.W. The high rock on the easterly side of Mount Nisbet is just over the house where we slept, and will be known in future as the Clachan. They say there are five kinds of wild animals on the mountains at the back, and but for these they could easily cross to Kupele. The Jakoni, Gomina, and Agila are very large and fierce. The Papara and Gadana are small, but fierce. We were eating biscuits, and they begged for a very small piece each, to keep as a charm to help them catch pigs. Hairs from the beard are in great demand as charms. Having seen all we wanted, and not being able to persuade the natives to accompany us up to the mountain to see the wild animals, I decided to return to

Orofedabe; so we returned to the village, gave the taro we bought to the people, paid our attendants and for the house where our things were, and away we went. Our friends were glad to see us, and rejoiced greatly when the taboo was taken off the salt, and taro was bought. We are having rain and thunderstorms every afternoon.

27*th*.—Maka poised a stick twelve feet long on his finger; the natives tried it and failed; again Maka did it, and all who were looking on came to the conclusion it was very easy for him to do, as a spirit held it for him. In each place we have been, when at prayers, all the natives are most respectful, keeping perfect silence and bending their heads. We had a fine tramp back to-day, and a refreshing bath in the Laroki after it. We have paid our carriers, and they are rejoicing greatly. We were glad to find our old friend and his wife well, and the things we left just as we hung them up. They are very anxious to have teachers here. We were telling them that we could see no people, and they have gone and brought in great crowds, saying, "No people! what are these?" I cut up tobacco and spread it out on a leaf in the centre of the crowd, and called out, "For Sogeri." One of their number was appointed by them, and he distributed it, all sitting quietly round. I got some salt in a paper, and did as with the tobacco. All rose, and in order approached, took some and retired, leaving the remainder, nearly half, for a very old man. The beads I gave to the women, the men saying they ought to have had them too. "Come and live with us; there is no place like Sogeri—it is good, it is large, it is peaceful, and there is plenty of food." So say the Sogerians. I was sitting on the ladder of the house, the crowd sitting round. Rua was in the bush with his gun; he fired at a bird, and it was amusing to see the simultaneous jerk of the crowd when they heard the shot.

28*th*.—Last night, a chief, Biaiori, of Eribagu, slept in the house with us, to be ready to lead us to his village and other villages about in the morning. We started about half-past seven; but it was evident at the start he had been talked over during the night in quiet whisperings, so as not to take us anywhere but his own village. We walked about a mile and a half, and came to his village, in a fine dry position, much preferable to the one we had left—good houses, one house floored with cedar slabs, and having a fine verandah all round. I wished to see a chief I had met yesterday, Jaroga, and was told he was at the next village, so we up with our bundles and away for about half a mile further on, to a nice clean village. I at once asked Jaroga to lead us to the places he named yesterday; he was quite willing, and began pointing in the various directions, and naming the villages, but was soon silenced by signs and words from others; he then said he could not go; so we left to go to Epakari; a young man very much attached to Maka, and who has been with us for ten days, having promised yesterday to lead us there. We had to carry our bags—not a very agreeable job. We had great excitement at leaving, our old chief insisting on our going back to Uakinumu; but we had discarded him, and were determined to find our own way should Someri, Maka's friend, fail us. I gave orders to keep a good look-out on Someri, who was carrying a bundle, and he was given into Maka's care. Our young friend was very quiet, and tried skulking behind and moving on fast ahead. When crossing a ridge about three miles from the village, I was leading, when we heard Maka calling for Someri. Rua at once returned, and found the bird had flown, leaving the bundle, but carrying with him the camp tomahawk, which Maka had foolishly let him have to cut a stick with. It would be folly to return to get the tomahawk, so we kept south and west for some distance, when we came to a deserted village; then we turned west. We crossed the Laroki several times before we came into the open country; at our last crossing we met a company of natives, all armed, on watch for Makapili natives, who were expected to attack them. They took our bundles, and led us to a small village, where we met some of our Marivaeanumu friends, who led us to their village and to our old house. A young child called Maka was presented for presents, the father telling Maka he called the child after him, because he was his friend when we were here last. We have now the open country before us, and expect no trouble in getting along. The natives are all unsettled at present, and every man we meet is armed. I can see the country better to-day than when here last week. Marivaeanumu is on a rise near the hills of Eikiri and north-north-west from Sogeri. The latter district is in a valley between the Owen Stanley Range and Mount Nisbet, to the south-west of it. Eribagu would make a good station for the Sogeri district. This place would be a suitable station being at the head of the plain that reaches away to the Astrolabe on the one side, and up to Vetura and Uakinumu on the other, stretching east by Mount Nisbet, and away east and south, by the country at the back of Mapakapa. The Laroki rises in the Owen Stanley Range, and is the drain for the Sogeri district and all the plain; it is very circuitous, and near here very deep and slow, flowing west.

29th.—For nearly six hours we have been travelling with our bags, and I can honestly say I feel tired. We are now at a new village—the houses just going up—on the top of the high green hill in front of Munikahila, overlooking the Kupa Moumiri valley. The village is named Keninumu, and consists of four houses at present, two on high trees and two on high rocks. We have pitched our tent close by, and intend resting until Monday, when we hope to start for the plain—a very fine country, but no natives. This part of the plain is dry and barren, with stunted gum-trees. A party met us when near the village, and a woman with a child on her shoulder, I suppose seeing me look tired, insisted on my giving her my bag. I looked at the child, and wondered how she was going to manage, but that was soon arranged; she made the child sit on her left shoulder, holding her by the hair; then she took my bundle, and away she went. Some young men have come in from one of the districts we wish to visit, and I hope to keep them until we leave; it will be a help and of great value as an introduction at this time of trouble. We are 1440 feet above sea-level.

A fortnight ago there was a great wallaby hunt down at Moumiri, and natives from all the districts round were present. A native of Munikahila speared a man from Tabori, who died soon after, so now Makipili, Epakari, and Efari are said to have joined on with Tabori, and unitedly mean to attack Munikahila. All the natives condemn the murder of the man, because of the time and place.

31st.—Natives all excitement, expecting Munikahila to be attacked. Every evening the men go armed to Munikahila, and the women, children, dogs, and pigs to the bush. I am sorry our Keninumu friends should consider it their duty to assist the murderers. The natives of the district to which the murdered man belonged are quietly biding their time, hunting wallaby close by us. The kind woman who assisted me the other day has a son by her first husband living at

Keninumu, and for a long time she has not seen him, he being afraid to come here. She knows that Maka was returning yesterday, and felt sure her son would accompany him. When some distance from here, Maka fired a shot, to let us know he was coming, to which we responded, assuring him all was right. On hearing the shot, the poor woman became quite excited, came and sat down by our fire, got up and got us firewood, sat down again, telling Kena to get the taro cooked for Maka, rose again and fetched more firewood, then sat down in front of the path, looking steadily and anxiously for the travellers. Poor body! they came in sight, but her son was not one of them. She seemed to feel it very much, rose, went to her house, and was not seen again until this morning. God grant the day is near when the song the heavenly host sang, "Glory to God in the highest, peace on earth and good will toward men," shall be known and enjoyed here!

September 1*st*.—We left this morning at seven o'clock and drew up at Makapili at four p.m., resting by the way. For salt, tobacco, and beads, we had help all the way. What appears a fine level plain in the distance turns out to be a fine country, full of ridges and luxuriant valleys, abounding in every kind of native vegetable. From the departure this morning until our bringing-up we could have ridden horses at a fine canter along the ridges from one to another. This is the best country I have yet seen in New Guinea, and the natives seem very kind and friendly. At the Laroki we had to strip, and, just above small rapids, holding on by a long line fastened to poles on each side, we crossed over. The natives have the line to help them when the river is up. We called at several villages on the ridges, passed others, some on large table-rocks. Fancy a table-rock with twenty or thirty houses on it. At Chokinumu, a village 1600 feet above the sea, S.E. from Marivaenumu seven miles, we alarmed the people so that they rushed away, leaving us the village. Shortly a man came back, pretending to be very unconcerned, chewing betel-nut; we soon were friends, and he called out to the others, and they returned. We told him where we were going, and he said he and his wife would accompany us, as we were the first foreigners who had ever been to his village, and he would not leave us. At other villages they also cleared out, screaming terribly. Gimenumu, 1900 feet above sea-level, and two miles east from Chokinumu, will make a fine mission station—a large village, fine plantations, and plenty of water. We crossed several streams from the Astrolabe Range, all flowing into the Laroki. The whole drainage of the Astrolabe Range and of this country falls into the Laroki. We are now in Vaiako, Makipili district, 2250 feet, in a really lovely spot.

There are a great many natives in this district. About four miles from here we passed a deserted village on a table-rock, at one time the home of this people; but the Sogeri natives came over and killed eleven of them, and the others thought it time to settle somewhere else. We have now a splendid view of Mount Owen Stanley, due north of us, and rising far away, clear and distinct above a thick mass of cloud. Mount Bellamy stands alone, with a bare south-east side, and Mount Nisbet just across from here, behind which is Sogeri, so much dreaded by this people. On all the ridges stretching away to the eastward from here behind Kapakapa are natives. A woman, coming to have a look at us, spied our black dog, Misi Dake, and off she went, climbing a tree, kit and all, quicker than I ever saw a native climb before. We met a fine old patriarch in a stream about two miles from here, and the meeting with our friend from Chokinumu was most affecting, touching chins and falling into one another's arms weeping. He sat down beside me with grave dignity, and the woman from Chokinumu sat in front of him, chanting and weeping. We had strawberries coming along, with little or none of the flavour of the home strawberry. The raspberry bush is very abundant.

2nd.—Just after sunrise we had a great crowd up at the tent to have a peep at us. At eight o'clock, we started for the summit of the Astrolabe, to have a look at the sea. It is very broken on the summit, and we had a good deal of ascending and descending before we got over Kaili, to be disappointed in not seeing the sea, the fog hanging thick under our feet. We returned by a very circuitous path, passing several villages built on rocks and trees. On one large table-rock was a snug village, and to the east of the rock four large posts beautifully carved. On feast days, the food is collected close to these, and a platform is fixed to the posts, on which dancing takes place. We returned at three p.m. The old chief soon followed us up to the camp with a large present of food, and saying he hoped we would soon return. I hope the same. After some delay, so that it might not appear as payment for the present, we gave our present to the old chief; when he got the tomahawk, he wept for joy, looked at his friends, then at us, pressed it to his bosom, and then kissed it. The chiefs name is Kunia.

3rd.—We left Makipili this morning at eight o'clock, and came along leisurely, arriving at Chokinumu at half-past ten. The chief and his wife who accompanied us pressed us to stay a night in their village, and, seeing it would displease them if we went on, we consented. We had a thorough downpour of rain in the afternoon, after a very hot sun, the thunder rolling all round us. The chief Lohiamalaka and his wife are exceedingly kind and attentive; they have kept close by us since we left here on Monday. I am sorry for the Makipili people; they are so afraid of Sogeri, that they have left their houses, and are living in the bush and under the shelter of rocks. Sogeri, Makipili says, will listen to no conditions of peace. Several overtures have been made, but all are useless. We were told at several places that if we ventured to Makipili we should never return; but we have been there, were treated kindly, and pressed to return.

4th.—Using our blankets yesterday as a flag for our tent, they got so wet that it required a day to dry them, so we decided to remain here and visit the Laroki Falls. Ten days ago, we found from the natives that they were near here. The native name is *Round*. We found the falls in a deep gorge formed by the west end of Astrolabe and east end of Vetura Range. On each side of the gorge the mountains run sharp down, in many places precipitous rocks. The falls are E. from Port Moresby, E.S.E. from Moumili, and S.E. from Vetura proper. They are grand, and well worth seeing. I wish we had seen them from below. For a long distance up there are small falls and rapids. The water comes surging on, and then takes a fearful leap of many hundred feet on to a ledge, and from there to the boiling cauldron below. The noise is deafening. Where we stood, nearly level with the water, it was 1340 feet above sea-level, and I do not think that from there to the cauldron could be less than 900 feet. I think it may be possible to get to them from the north side by Mangara, and then we can rightly tell the height of the falls.

5th.—Left Chokinumu this morning at eight, and had a pleasant walk for three hours, ascending gradually the Astrolabe until we reached the summit at the back of Tupuselei, 2300 feet high. We were resting before descending, when a native party appeared and approached us, somewhat scared. They said on coming up they heard the noise as of chopping wood (we were marking trees). They came on, and saw through the bush a white man, and at once went back; then, hearing as if natives were with him speaking in Koiari, they returned and determined to meet. They were much pleased at receiving a present of salt. We descended on the west side of the Astrolabe; the descent, being steep and difficult, took us some time. In the afternoon we arrived at Janara, near to Efari, at the back of Pyramid Point, the Astrolabe bearing north. Our friend Lohiamalaka, the chief of Geminumu Monito, and three youths are with us. I have never met a kinder and more friendly native than Lohiamalaka. Janara is a good large district, and seems to have a number of natives. The village we are in is 600 feet above sea-level. Tupuselei is the nearest mission station, and a teacher placed here or at Efari would have constant communication with that place. I was the first to enter the village. They had heard us cooeying to one another; so only saw one man, and he tried to look very unconcerned, with a bamboo pipe, trying to light it, but too excited to succeed. The women had shut themselves indoors with the children, and the men had gone into the bush close by with their weapons.

6th.—From Janara to Epakari there are several steep ridges to go up and down, and the last ascent is truly steep. It took us three good steady hours' walking and climbing to get to Karikatana, the first of six villages in this district. Dawes and Stone were at a village, I believe, on a ridge nearer to Port Moresby. The chief, Nikanivaipua, received us graciously, and insisted on our taking his house. We paid off our friends, and they departed well pleased. We received presents of cooked food and smoked wallaby. They were prepared for us, having been shouted to an hour before we arrived at the village by our friend Lohiamalaka. The village looks to be in a fine healthy position, close to the west end of the Astrolabe, the high bluff bearing N.E. They have plenty of all kinds of food. We crossed from the Janara, a good-sized mountain torrent flowing S.W. to Bootless Inlet. We are 700 feet high. High bluff of Astrolabe, N.E.; Bootless Inlet, S.S.W.; peak of Astrolabe above Kaili, E.S.E.

7th.—Our friend Lohiamalaka turned up again last evening; he did not like leaving us. This morning he really set off, promising to visit us at Port Moresby in October; that is, not this moon, nor the next, but the one that follows. I asked for a little ginger to eat, and they have brought it me in bundles. It is really good when green, with salt. A large number of natives attended our service, and were truly orderly—not a whisper, and during prayer every head bent. On the Astrolabe, the other day, Lohiamalaka said he felt anxious for us in entering Janara. Rua, through Kena, told him not to fear anything on our account, as the Great Spirit was with us, and no harm could come near us. Last evening, he was telling the people here of his fears, and what Rua said, "and how true it was the Great Spirit or something is with them." At all the villages Lohiamalaka repeated all he could remember of what he had been told, and of our singing and praying. Every evening he would sit at the tent door and get us to sing for the benefit of a crowd of natives outside, who, having heard from himself of our musical powers, refused to go to their homes at sunset, and insisted on remaining until after *noko* (singing). When the Koiari visit the coast they go in for begging largely, and they generally get what they ask, as the Motu people are very much afraid of their spiritual power, they being thought to hold power over the sun, wind, and rain, and manufacturing or withholding the latter at will. When the Motu people hear that Koiarians are coming, they hide their valuables. All the young swells here have head-dresses of dogs' teeth, got from the seaside natives. At Eikiri, they told us they got theirs by killing and stealing. We can truly say we are under arms in this house—sixty-two spears overhead, four shields on walls, and two stone clubs keeping watch at the door. A Makipili woman has been telling Kena how she happens to be here. Formerly her people and these were at enmity. Makipili sought peace, but had no pig. She was selected to supply want of pig, and taken with food. When she grew up, the old man (not her husband) insisted on her living with him.

8th.—We had six hours' good walking, and are now encamped under the shade of Vetura. The country from Epakari to here is very ridgy, and, after leaving the ridges of Epakari, very barren. Coming suddenly on a large party of men, women, and children returning from a dance, they were so frightened when we called out, *Naimo*! that they set off, kits, spears, and drums, and no fine words would bring them back. We have seven natives with us; the old chief says he must see us safe to Keninumu. We passed a fine village—Umiakurape—on a ridge west of Karikatana; the chiefs name is Vaniakoeta. It would make a splendid station. The high ridge at the back of Epakari, along which we came, is 1000 feet high, and from it we saw Fisherman's Island, Redscar Bay, Bootless Inlet, and the whole coast east to Round Head.

9th.—Arrived at Keninumu at half-past ten a.m. Found all well. The natives are constantly on the look-out for the Tabori attack on Munikahila. We hear the Munikahila natives have been stealing from Goldie.

14th.—Since our return we have been house-building, but are getting on very slowly. I fear we are six weeks too late for the Kupele district, and shall have to leave it for another season. It would be awkward to get in and not get back until the end of the wet season. I find our friend the chief, Poroko, has had two wives; one he killed lately. She was in the plantation, and some young fellows coming along, she sat down with them to have a smoke and get the news; Poroko heard of it, and on her coming home in the evening he killed her. A woman at Favelle said, "Oh, the Koiari man thinks nothing of killing his wife." The word for "sneeze" in Koiari is *akiso*. When they are leaving for a journey or going for the night they call out *kiso*, and often from their houses they shout their good-night to us, *kiso*. There is a woman in deep mourning for her daughter. She has hanging round her neck all the ornaments once the property of the deceased, and along with them the jawbone. The headless body she visits occasionally, and rubs herself all over with the juice from it!

18*th*.—We have a great crowd of natives in from Kupele, the nearest district to Mount Owen Stanley. They are the same race of people as at Meroka—some very dark, others very light-coloured. Their weapons are the same as the Koiari, as also is their dress. Two men are in mourning, and are wearing netted vests. The chief is rather a fine-looking fellow, and dressed profusely with cassowary feathers. They all have a wisp of grass bound tight at one end, and hanging from a girdle behind, to be used as a seat when they sit down. It is a stretch of imagination to say it looks like a tail. They are very anxious we should accompany them on their return, and say they will show us plenty of villages and people. Yesterday we had great feasting in the villages on yams and taro. To an Eastern Polynesian it would be ridiculous to call it a feast, seeing there was no pig. In the evening we had a good deal of palavering with spears and shields, fighting an imaginary foe, and at times retreating. Their movements are swift and graceful: advance, retreat, advance, pursue, ward off to the right, to the left, shield up, down, aside, struck on knee, a shout, all gone through, with the greatest alacrity, and I am not at all astonished at so few being killed or wounded in a fight. They value shields that bear the marks of spears.

19*th*.—Our old friend Oriope came in to-day, and handed us the tomahawk, stolen by the deserter on our last trip. He says when he heard how Someri had served us he sent at once to Sogeri, and got the tomahawk, telling them it was very wrong to steal from such dear friends of his. One of the Kupele natives stole a knife, but he had to give it up to the Keninumu friends, who returned it to us. I should have liked to have started a station at Chokinumu, so as to try the climate of both sides of the district this wet season.

23*rd*.—We find it impossible to get the men to help us with the house whilst so many of us are here, so we return to the port, hoping to get into Chokinumu soon. The people, seeing that we are really going, have begged hard for Jakoba to be left, and they promise faithfully to assist him in finishing the house. Jakoba being anxious to remain with them, I consented.

24*th*.—Arrived at Moumiri about two p.m. We heard there that Tabori and Makipili have been murdering. A number of people from

Marivaenumu were here wallaby-hunting, and on returning were met; three women and two men were killed. They report here, also, that Kupele proper (a small village) no longer exists; the Koiari to the west of us having gone over and killed all but five, who have gone to another village.

26th.—Returned to Port Moresby to-day, and found all well, and good news from all the stations. The services have gone on here in Rua's absence with great success. On two Sundays the chief Poi conducted the services, addressing those present, and telling them he thought that now it was time for them all to receive the Gospel which had been so faithfully taught them during these years; in prayer he remembered us who were inland, and asked our Father in heaven to watch over us and bring us back safely, and to enlighten all of them at the seaside.

CHAPTER IV
PEACE-MAKING

Mr. Chalmers asked by the natives to go to Elema—Native fears—Difficulties at the start—Namoa—Delena—A Motumotu trading canoe—Interview with Semese, chief of Lese—Christian natives—Friendly meeting with a war canoe—Arrival at Motumotu—Friendly reception—Viewing Mr. Chalmers's feet—Natives in full dress—Sunday open-air service—Sago as an article of commerce—Peace agreed upon—Return to Boera.

When at Kabadi in 1880, the natives begged of me to endeavour to prevent the Elema natives paying them another visit, as they were now living in the bush near the hills. All along the coast the people were much afraid, expecting a raid, and at last news came in from Maiva that Motumotu and Lese were making great preparations that they would visit Motu, kill Tamate and Ruatoka, then attack right and left. Last year, when leaving, they said they would return and pay off accounts, kill the foreigners first, then all the natives they could get hold of.

Under these circumstances, I resolve to visit Motumotu, and beard the lion in his den. I did not believe they would touch me, but I feared they meant mischief to Kabadi and the coast villages. No time could be lost, as we were in a bad month for rain and storms, and the coast line is long and bad. The natives said it was too late, yet I resolved to try it.

On the 5th January, 1881, we opened the new church at Port Moresby, and baptised the first three New Guinea converts. The church was crowded, and all seemed interested. I arranged for Piri and his wife to accompany me to the Gulf, they taking the whale-boat. We cannot call at Kabadi on our way down, as we must hurry on, but our natives here were going to Kabadi, and gladly took the news.

On January 10, the flag flying on the boat told all that we were to start. Our leader ran off to Kaili last night, but Huakonio, one of the three baptised on the 5th, was willing to go. Our boat's crew were considered fools, rushing into the arms of death. Wives, children, and friends were gathered round weeping. The men said, "Cannot you see that if Tamate lives we shall live, and if he is murdered we shall be murdered? It is all right; we are going with him, and you will see us back all right with sago and betel-nuts." Huakonio told me in the boat that every means imaginable but physical force were used to prevent their accompanying me; and he added, "We know it is all right; the Spirit that has watched over you in the past" (naming the various journeys) "will do so now; and if we return safe, won't the people be ashamed?"

We left Port Moresby about nine a.m. with a light head wind; outside found the current very strong, setting easterly. We arrived at Boera at four p.m., and found Piri and his wife ready to start at once. Piri has a Boera crew, and we increased ours here by two. Here the natives did not seem at all afraid, and many wished to accompany us.

On leaving Boera, it was a beautiful clear and moonlight night, and there was a light land breeze. Pulling brought us to Varivara Islands, in Redscar Bay, about two a.m., where we anchored until six when we tried to make Cape Suckling. As it was blowing hard from the north-west, we had to put into Manumanu. The Motu traders did all they could to persuade us to give up Motumotu, and to visit Kabadi. Both crews would gladly have given up; their friends told them to leave us, and return in the trading canoes. They came to me to say "the bad weather has set in, the winds and rains are here, we cannot go on."

I replied, "Think, my children, of the disgrace. We started to go to Motumotu, and at the first breath of contrary wind we put back. It must not be. Let us try it a little longer, and if the wind increases we can put back, and not feel ashamed."

"You are right," they rejoined; "we will go on with you."

At sunset we all got into our boats, and were ready for a start. A fellow who has just returned from Kabadi thought to get over me by saying, "Tamate, Kabadi are looking daily for you, and they have a large present ready; feathers in abundance and sago; your two boats cannot take half."

"I am going to Motumotu, and not all the feathers in Kabadi, nor all the sago they can prepare, will turn me now, until I have made a fair trial, and then, if driven back, I will visit Kabadi."

I believe our crew had had a talk with that man before he came to me.

It was five o'clock on January 12th before we got to Namoa, near Cape Suckling. Maiva canoes passed with wallaby from Namoa. When ashore, cooking breakfast, Koloko and her husband, with uncles and aunts, and men and women from the village, came down. The two former were going to Maiva, and the crowd followed to see them embark in one of the large Maiva canoes. After the bamboo pipe had been passed all round, the embarkation took place, men and women weeping as if taking a final farewell.

When they had gone, we told the people we wished to sleep, and they left us undisturbed. In the afternoon we came to Delena, where we had right hearty welcome. They are truly glad we are going to Motumotu, as they fear an attack, and hope our visit will benefit them. They feel sure Motumotu will receive us well, and seeing that I specially visit them, they say it will be all right. The crews feel encouraged, and are at present ashore feasting on dugong, sago, and betel-nuts. Some have been off for tobacco, and are now laughing at the folly of their friends. The sorcerer is not in Delena; but even he would do nothing to prevent our going on. We are all ready to start with a land breeze. The crews have sent us word, "When you wish to start, call out; you will see us gladly spring into the water."

On leaving Delena with a light breeze and pulling, we reached the Kaveri beach near Cape Possession, about eight a.m. When near Maiva, we met a Motumotu canoe. At first they were afraid to come alongside of us, but after a little talk we got near them, exchanged presents, and were soon friends. They seem glad we are going to their home; they say peace will be arranged. The Motumotu have said that if we only were to visit them, they would gladly make peace.

It seems that they are very badly off for *uros* (earthenware pots), and the native tribes along the coast to the west of them are crying out and blaming them for the scarcity. They are certainly blaming the right party; but for Motumotu, the Pari, Vapukori, Port Moresby, Boliapata, and Boera trading canoes would all have been down the coast last season. The principal man in the canoe, knowing that all, except our boatman, Bob Samoa, had friends at Motumotu, made friends with him, rubbing noses and handing his lime gourd, which is to be shown on arrival, and his father and friends will receive Bob as his friends. They go on to Lolo in quest of *uros*.

We landed to cook food. On awaking from a sleep, I was astonished to find a crowd of natives close by, and my friend the Kaveri chief, Arana, sitting near me. Two boys, who were on the beach fishing, seeing us land, ran inland and reported, and he, with two of his wives carrying food, followed by men and women from the villages, came down. His two wives are now busy cooking, and he is trying to persuade me to call on our return and get his present of sago and food. I could not promise, and he seemed disappointed.

We left the Kaveri beach and pulled round Cape Possession, passing close in by Oiapu. A heavy sea was rolling in, and a canoe putting off to us was swamped. People running along the beach called on Piri and me by name to land and feast, but our crews were too frightened, and we went on. When off Jokea, men, women, and children all came on to the beach, and also by name begged of us to land. We would have done so here, but the sea was too high, breaking with great force on the fringing reef. Several canoes put off, but only one succeeded in reaching us. They begged of us to call on our return, and let them know the result of our visit, and said we had better also visit Lese. They think our visit will put all straight. Motumotu, they say, is very undecided as to what to do, but having heard that I was to visit them, put off the decision for some time, saying, "If he comes, it will be all right, and we shall have peace, but—" Well, they did not know. They rub noses all round, and make for the shore, we for the harbour at the mouth of Coombes River, but a very heavy sea running in, we prefer anchoring outside at midnight.

By five a.m. up anchor, and away to Lese. Two Naima canoes returning from Lolo, where they had been trying to get *uros*, passed close to us. They also are glad of the likelihood of peace and *uros*. At seven, we got to Lese, and were met by an excited crowd, the majority armed. We anchored a little out, and would allow no canoes alongside. I called out for Eeka, and a very old man walked into the sea, when I went ashore and took him by the hand. Piri and his wife followed, with part of the crew and the Boera and Port Moresby chiefs. We were led to the village, the crowd increasing as we went along. Piri noticing an enclosed place, went in to see what it was, and called me to have a look. I went in, but no women or youths followed. Inside were two large houses, with rows of masks and hats, the latter like small canoes, about ten feet long, made with very light wood and native cloth. On coming out I was seized by the hand by an elderly man, who, in a towering passion, drew me on. All I could make out was that somebody was a thief and a liar. The Boera chief ran up, and I asked him what was wrong. "Oh, this is your friend, Semese, the chief you gave the present to when you were last here, and he is angry with Eeka for taking you away."

"Tell Piri to come up quickly."

"Piri, go with Eeka as your friend; give him a present as such; it is all right. I go with Semese."

Soon squatting on the platform, wrath fled, and I had to wait to be fed.

"But, Semese, I want to press on to Motumotu and see them. I am afraid of the weather coming on bad."

"Motumotu to-morrow, Lese to-day; you must have a pig."

"Leave the pig for another visit."

All was of no avail. A fine pig was speared, brought and laid at my feet. Semese and the people were in the very best humour. Eeka was delighted with Piri, and the latter had a pig presented to him. We gave our presents, and, feeling tired, I suggested to our friends that we had better take the pigs to the other side of the entrance, to Macey Lagoon. Semese is quite agreeable, now the peace is made, and it was arranged that he and his party should visit me with sago at Port Moresby. Both pigs, ready for cooking, were carried into the boat, and the excited crowd, this time all unarmed, were on the shore to see us off. They promised not to molest Kabadi again, and that they considered our visit as peace with all the coast villages.

Macey Lagoon would make a splendid harbour for small vessels, very large vessels not being able to cross the bar. On the eastern side, a bank runs out for nearly a mile, on which the sea breaks; close in by western shore is a good passage. The great work of the day was feasting and sleeping. There were two Lese men with us, and they said that the Motumotu have been talking of war, not of peace; but now it may be different. To get into Motumotu in the morning, we had come to within two miles of the village, and we anchored off. Notwithstanding some anxiety, soon all were asleep. The natives were astonished at the beautiful weather, and said they felt as if all would be right—the great and good Spirit who had led us so far and safely would not leave us now or on the morrow. At every meal on board or ashore they asked a blessing, and our old friend Hula prayed with real earnest feelings. He was certainly in earnest to-night when he prayed for the Motumotuans, and that our visit might be blessed to them. I was charmed with his simplicity, fervour, and expectancy.

This old man, a few weeks before, at the close of a meeting at Port Moresby, said, addressing *us*—

"Listen, you think we Motumotuans are not attending to your words; but you are mistaken. Before you came here, we were always fighting and were a terror to all, east and west, but now it is different. We are at peace all round; we go about unarmed, and sleep well at night. Soon our fathers' ancient customs will be given up, and you will see us, old and young, coming to be taught the word of the great and good Spirit."

I was aroused about two a.m. by shouting, and, looking over the gunwale, saw a large double fighting canoe alongside of Piri's boat, in which all were sound asleep. On awaking, they were startled by the appearance. They were asked by those on the bridge—

"Who are you?"

"Tamate and Piri going to Motumotu."

Soon all were friends, chewing betel-nut and smoking tobacco. On each canoe with paddles were over thirty men, and on the bridge adjoining the canoes were armed men and a large supply of sago and betel-nuts. They were going to Lese to purchase *uros*. They came alongside of our boat, received and gave presents, and then an order was given by one from the bridge, and away they went at full speed. It was a pretty sight in the moonlight to see the canoe move swiftly on, when nearly eight paddles as one touched the water. We rolled ourselves up again for another hour or two's sleep.

At sis a.m. we weighed anchor, and were off to Motumotu. There was a great crowd on the beach; but it was all right, as boys and girls were to be seen there, as noisy as the grown-up folks. A chief rushed into the water, and called on us to come. "Come, with peace from afar; come, friends, and you will meet us as friends." We went round and entered the river in deep water, close to eastern bank near to the village. Until we had a talk, I would allow none but Piri's friend and my friends, Semese and Rahe, near the boats. They had been told that we were going to fight if they visited us, and that all women and children were to be sent back to the Keiara, and the Keiari fighting men were to be in league with all the foreigners about. Then they heard that I had been murdered, and were terribly sorry; but now they saw I was alive, and had come a long way in a "moon" in which neither they nor their forefathers had ever travelled. So now they must make peace.

I said, "You must not again go near Kabadi, and all along the coast we must have peace."

"It is right, we shall not again visit Kabadi. Lealea feasted us with pigs, and pressed us to attack Kabadi, to pay off an old attack on them. It suited us, because Kabadi thought themselves strong; but now it is peace."

I landed with them, and went up through the villages, then returning to the boats we were told to remain there. Shortly three pigs were brought, and our return presents of *uros*, etc., were carried off. Bob's calabash has brought him a host of friends. Piri is with his friends at one end of the village, and in the opposite I am to reside in my friend Rahe's *dubu*. Semese is his father, and a very old man. The number of old men and old women and children is astonishing. No enemy dare come near their villages, and their houses have never been burnt down. The Boera chief—a capital fellow to have—speaks this dialect very fluently. Our people at first were very much afraid, but soon settled down, and are now roving about.

Suddenly the war-horn was heard blowing—not the pig-horn, so often heard on the coast. I wondered what was up, but it turned out to be only the youth training. Two new double canoes came down the river with large complements of paddles, all young lads, gaily dressed. A number of young men, painted and extravagantly dressed, have been here; they lately killed some Moveavans, and are hence greatly admired by old and young.

I had to take off my boots and socks, and allow my feet to be admired, also to show off my chest. All shout with delight, and every new arrival must have a look. The sun was frightfully hot. Some men were fishing on the breakers; they had a long post, with a cross-bar, on which they stand, fixed in the sand, head covered with native cloth, and bow and arrow ready.

A number of people came in from Vailala. They wish I would go down with them, but it is too late to go so far in an open boat. I have had another meeting with the leading men, and I think all is now peace. My friend Rahe seems a great personage, with relatives innumerable. He wants to know if I would like to be alone in the *dubu*; only say it, and all the men will leave. I prefer them remaining, and I will make myself comfortable on the front platform.

In the evening, men and women—I suppose *they* would say "elegantly dressed"—bodies besmeared with red pigment, croton and *dracæna* leaves, and feathers of various birds fixed on head, arms, and legs, paraded the villages. At present all move about armed, and in this establishment bows, bent and unbent, and bundles of arrows are on all sides.

Rahe has just been to me to ask for boat medicine.

"What do you mean, Rahe?"

"I want you to give me some of that medicine you use to make your boat sail."

"I use no medicine, only Motu strong arms."

"You could never have come along now without medicine."

"We use no medicine, and have come along well."

I had a splendid night's rest. My mosquito-net and blanket caused great amusement. My attendants are innumerable and attentive, and will allow no noise near. Our service in the morning was very noisy—everybody anxious for quiet must needs tell his neighbour to be quiet. Our old Port Moresby chief prayed in the Motumotu dialect. The Boera chief translated for Piri and me. They are very anxious to know of the resurrection and where Beritane spirits go after death.

In the afternoon we held service in the main street. The singing attracted a very large and noisy crowd but when our old friend began to pray it was as if a bomb-shell had exploded, men, women, and children running as for dear life to their homes. Another hymn brought them back, armed and unarmed. We had a long talk on peace, and they wished I would go with them to Moveave, and make peace. One division of these villages they have simply wiped out. I asked them to leave Moveave alone, and when a fit season comes I will ascend the river with them, and make peace.

I have visited the party who last week killed several of the Moveavans, and they promised not to attack them again. The Kaback jewellery is about in abundance.

Semese spoke nearly all the night through, exhorting all to peace, and that now we had visited them they ought no more to go about exalting themselves, fighting with their neighbours, and speaking evil of their friends, the Motuans. Rahe has brought his son, whom he has named Tamate. I have no doubt he will be an expensive honour.

We went up the William River to-day. At mouth, on the west side, are two islands, viz., Iriho and Biaveveka. Between the latter and the mainland is an entrance into Alice Meade Harbour. The river is broad and deep. Both banks are lined with sago palms.

When a young man marries a young woman, the custom here is to pay nothing for her; but for a widow something very great. The people live chiefly on sago. Sago is cooked with shell-fish, boiled with bananas, roasted on stones, baked in the ashes, tied up in leaves, and many other ways. We have received large presents of sago, both boats bearing as much as is safe to carry. We leave in the morning. At present a man is going through the streets in great wrath, having been to his plantation and missed a bunch of bananas. As he moves along he shouts out his loss, and challenges the thief.

We had a gathering of old men until late into the night, and they closed with a wail, chanted, with drums keeping time. Hours before daylight Semese was up, waiting for me to turn out.

We had a fine run back to Yule, where, at sunset, we were met by a terrific gale of wind and a thunderstorm. We had to put in close to the land, and for four hours sit it out in a deluge of rain. It was soon inky dark, the lightning very vivid, and the thunder deafening. Piri's boat anchored close alongside. On the weather clearing up a little, we crossed Hall Sound to Delena, where we were soon met by natives carrying torches, and were led to their houses. A change of clothing, and we were all as comfortable as possible.

We spent the hour of midnight with Kone and Levas, chiefs of Delena, telling them of our visit to the west, and its success in establishing peace. They were greatly delighted, and will do me the honour of visiting me at Port Moresby, that is, will relieve me of some tomahawks. With a light wind and a smooth sea, we had a pleasant run to Boera, where we arrived at sunset. There was great joy in the village at our arrival.

We reached Port Moresby on the 20th, and on March 6th we baptized Kohu and Rahela, the first two women of New Guinea converted to Christianity. May they be kept as true ministering women for Christ!

CHAPTER V
THE KALO MASSACRE

Twelve teachers and their friends killed at Kalo in 1881—The warning—The massacre—The fear for the teachers at Koma—Mr. Chalmers's views on the question—Voyage westwards in the *Mayri*—A Sunday at Delena—Visit of Queen Koloka—Threatened attack by Lolo natives—The fight—Peace—Miria's village—Bad character of the Motu natives—Visit to the chief of Motu Lavao—Story of Dr. Thorngren's murder—Peace made with the village.

On the 7th of March, 1881, the natives of Kalo, a village at the head of Hood Bay, near the mouth of the Kemp Welch River, massacred their teacher, Anederea, with his wife and two children; also Materua, teacher of Kerepunu, his wife and two children; Taria, teacher of Hula; Matatuhi, an inland teacher; and two Hula boys—in all, twelve persons.

The earliest news of the tragedy was given in the following letter from the Rev. T. Beswick, dated Thursday Island, Torres Straits, March 24th:—

> On Friday, the 4th inst., Taria, our Hula teacher, left Port Moresby with Matatuhi, an inland teacher, the latter wishing to visit the Kalo teacher for some native medicine. Reaching Hula on the evening of the 4th, Taria heard a rumour that the Kalo people intended to kill their teacher and his family. Accordingly he went thither the following day, along with Matatuhi, and requested the Kalo teacher and his family to leave at once. The teacher refused to place credence in the rumour, and even questioned his chief and pretended friend, who assured him that there was not the slightest grain of truth in the rumour.
>
> The Hula teacher returned, leaving Matatuhi behind. On Monday, the 7th, Taria, along with five

Hula boys, proceeded in a boat to Kalo and Kerepunu, with the view of bringing the teachers and their families to Hula, on account of the ill-health of some of the party. He called at Kalo on the way thither, and apprised the teacher of his intention to call on the return journey. At Kerepunu he took on board the teacher, his wife and two children, and one native youth. The party then proceeded to Kalo. During the interval of waiting there, the chief and pretended friend of the Kalo teacher got into the boat for a chat. On the arrival of Matatchi and the Kalo teacher, along with his wife and two children, the chief stepped out of the boat. This was the pre-arranged signal for attack to the crowds assembled on the bank. At the outset, the chief warned his followers not to injure the Hula and Kerepunu boys; but such precaution did not prevent two of the former being killed. The other four boys escaped by swimming the river. The mission party were so cooped up in the boat, and spears flew so thickly and fast, as to render resistance futile and escape impossible. Taria resisted for a time, but a fourth spear put an end to his resistance. The others were dispatched with little trouble. A single spear slew both mother and babe in the case of both women. The only bodies recovered were those of the Kerepunu teacher's wife and her babe; the natives of Hula and Kerepunu severally interred the two bodies. The rest of the bodies became a prey to the alligators. For the two Hula boys who were slain speedy compensation was made by the Kalo people. The whale-boat, too, was recovered by the Hula natives.

The above sad intelligence reached Port Moresby at early morn of the 11th, just as the *Harriet* was about to leave for Thursday Island, and the *Mayri* about to take me to Hula, whilst a party of foreigners were leaving for the East End. The news, of course, upset all arrangements, and, after the first moments of excitement were over, our next concern was about the safety of the two Aroma teachers. With as little delay as possible, but with groundless forebodings of coming evil, a large party of us left for Aroma. About ten a.m. of the 14th, we reached there, and whilst our three boats lay off a little, so as not to arouse suspicion, a teacher and myself went ashore. With devout gratitude I heard that both teachers and natives were ignorant of the massacre. In less than an hour the two teachers and their families were safely ensconced in their whale-boat, taking along with them but a minimum of their property, according to the orders given. By these means the chiefs and natives of Aroma were left in utter ignorance as to the cause of our erratic movements, nor did they seem to suspect anything.

At Kerepunu we experienced considerable noise and worry. Here, too, we judged it prudent to remove very little belonging to the deceased teacher. At Hula, my house had been entered, but the few things stolen were mostly returned. Here, too, we have left goods, until some definite course be decided upon. Strange to say, at Hula, where we expected the least trouble and danger, there we had the greatest; indeed, on one or two occasions, affairs assumed a rather serious aspect. The main idea present in the native mind was to take advantage of us in our weakness and sorrow. After a very brief stay at Hula, we left there on the 15th, reaching Port Moresby the following day; and on the 17th I left for Thursday Island.

The natives of Hood Bay attribute this massacre to the influence of Koapina, the Aroma chief, he having assured the Kalo people that foreigners might be massacred with impunity, citing as an illustration the massacre at Aroma last July, and pointing out at the same time the great fame that had thereby accrued to his own people. The Kalo people have not been slow in acting upon his advice. I visited Hula and Kerepunu within six weeks of the massacre, and was so impressed with the peaceful bearing of the people in both places that I should have been glad to have re-occupied both stations immediately.

I should have visited Kalo, but was afraid of compromising the mission, as it is possible the natives may be punished for the outrage. I fear we are not altogether free from blame; the teachers are often very indiscreet in their dealings with the natives, and not over-careful in what they say; there has also, perhaps, sometimes been a niggard regard to expense on our part. A very few pounds spent at a station like Kalo in the first years would, I believe, prevent much trouble, and probably murder. The Kalo natives felt that Hula and Kerepunu got the most tobacco and tomahawks, and that their share was small indeed. Instead of our buying all the thatch required for the other stations—only obtainable at Kalo—we got the teachers, with their boys, to get it. We meant it well, to save expense. My experience teaches me to throw all I can in the way of natives not connected with our head station. At this station—Port Moresby—for the next few years the expenses will be considerable in buildings, laying out the land, and in presents to the constant stream of visitors; but it will have a Christianizing and a civilizing effect upon a large extent of country.

On the 24th of May, 1881, left Port Moresby in the *Mayri*, and, having taken on board four natives at Boera, continued a westerly course, anchoring next day in Hall Sound, opposite Delena. Early on the morning of May 26th, Kone and Lavao, our old friends, came off. They say it is useless going to Maiva, as we cannot land; but we can go and see for ourselves, and they will accompany us. I had to land to eat pigs, *i.e.*, receive pigs and hand them over to my followers. On landing, they led me up the hill at the back of village, where I was astonished to find a fine tract of land forming a splendid position for a house. Kone at once offered me as much land as I wanted. After thinking it over on board, I decided on building. I landed tents, and pitched them on the rise above the village. My experience is that places quite exposed to south-east wind are *more* unhealthy than swampy country. On Rarotonga there were more deaths on the windward side of the island than on the leeward.

On the Sunday after landing, we went down and had service in the village. Kone interpreted into Lolo. When telling the people we had no work for them on Sunday, Kone said: "Oh! we know, and we, too, are going to be *helaka* (sacred) to-morrow." I asked him, "Come, Kone, how do you know?" "From Boera." I met a lad repeating the Lord's Prayer in Motu, and found he had been taught by Piri. The Motu tribe has already had great influence, and will have more and more every year. I have an interesting class of children, and hope, before we leave, they will know their letters well.

What nonsense one could write of the reception here—such as "Everybody at service this morning listened attentively; commented on address or conversation; children all come to school, so intelligent,

and seemingly anxious to learn; and, altogether, prospects are bright."
At home they would say, why, they are being converted; see the
speedy triumph! Alas! they are but savages, pure and simple, rejoicing
in the prospect of an unlimited supply of tobacco, beads, and
tomahawks.

Paura, a chief from Motu Lavao, is in. The people, it seems, told
him, being *helaka* day, I could not meet him, and he did not come up
hill. He is rather a nice-looking fellow, with a mild, open
countenance. Kone told him to tell the Paitana natives, who
murdered James and Thorngren, that, if they wished peace and
friendship, they must come in here and sue for it; that I could not first
go to them, as they were the offenders and murderers.

Arrangements were at once made for erecting a wooden house at
Delena, measuring thirty-six feet by eighteen feet, material for which
was easily procurable. On the 30th of May, Queen Koloka, her
husband, and a number of men and women came in. The Prince
Consort first came up, all over smiles, followed in half an hour by his
wife and maids. After formally receiving her, I presented Mrs.
Lawes's present. I unloosed the parcel, and turned maid-of-honour in
real waiting. Her Majesty was chewing betel-nut, but that did not
prevent my putting the dress on; first attempt all wrong, the front
became the back, and the back the front. At length I succeeded, and,
after fastening the dress, tied a pretty kerchief round the royal neck.
There was great excitement, in every mouth a thumb, a few moments
of silence, and then every soul spoke and shouted. It was amusing to
see her husband, uncles, maids, old men and women, young men and
maidens, gather round the royal presence, wonder and admire, and
then shout, *Oh misi haine O!* (Mrs. Lawes). Ah, Koloka, I wonder how
you are going to get out of that dress to-night; will you understand
buttons, hooks, and eyes?

During my stay at Delena, one of those warlike incursions by
hostile tribes so common in New Guinea took place. My presence
and influence happily brought about an early and satisfactory
settlement of the dispute. I extract the following from my journal:—

June 2nd.—Our friends seem troubled, and their house-building earnestness is somewhat abated. I find they have heard that the Lolo tribe intend making a raid on them. Is it on them, or on us? Their great hope is that we shall use our guns, and so frighten the invaders. I tell them that we cannot do this; that we are men of peace, and have no wish to frighten any one. It seems Maiva is very disturbed; they are fighting all round, avenging Oa's death, and may soon be expected here. Maiva would not interfere with us, but Lolo I would not trust.

We shall have to keep a good look-out to-night. Our friends seem very troubled and excited. I have given warning that any one coming near our camp must call out my name and his or her own. No one can come near without our knowing, as my terrier Flora is a splendid watch-dog. This evening, some women passed camp, carrying their valuables to hide away in the bush. Bob asks, "Suppose Lolo natives come to us, what we do?" "Of course they will not come near to us unless they mean to attack, and then we must defend ourselves." The guns are ready. It is not pleasant; but I fancy they will not molest us, so hope to sleep well, knowing we are well cared for by Him who is never far off. Through much trouble we get to be known, and the purpose for which we come is understood.

3rd.—Last night I slept lightly, with Flora on watch, and Bob easily aroused. After midnight he kept watch. We placed the lights beyond tents on each side, and so arranged that the light would strike on any native nearing camp. About two a.m. Lavao's wife No. 2 came up with her grandchild, goods, and chattels for safety. The Loloans were coming. All right; all ready. Very loud, noisy talking in village. At four, we called out for Kone, who came up telling us that we should be first disposed of, then Delena. I went to the village, and saw the old friendly chief from Lavao. I told him any Loloan coming over the brow of the hill with weapons we should consider as coming to fight, and we were ready. At five, women and children crowded into camp, with all their belongings, and asked for protection. Certainly; we shall do what we can for them. Men are running all about, planting arms in convenient places in the bush. We are told to keep a good look-out— and that we shall. It is now daylight, so we do not care much. The fight has begun in the village. Some Loloans, running after Delena natives, rush uphill; we warn them back, and they retire. There is a loud shout for us to go to the village and fight. I leave Bob with guns and cartridges to keep watch over camp. I have more confidence in the skirmish unarmed, and have no wish for the savages to think I have come to fight. I shout out *Maino*, and soon there is a hush in the terrible storm. I am allowed to walk through the village, disarm one or two, and, on my return to our friend Kone's end of the village, he whispers to me, "There is Arua," understanding him to mean the chief, or *vata tauna* (sorcerer). I recognize in him the man introduced to me on a former visit, and who in wrath cleared out from my presence. Now might be his time to pay me out. I take his weapons from him, link him on to me, and walk him up the hill. I speak kindly to him, show him flag, and tell him we are *maino*, and warn him that his people must on no account ascend the hill. All right, he will stop the fighting. I sit down to write this, when again they rush up for me, saying Kone was to be killed. Leaving Bob with arms in charge, I go down to the village, and without my hat. More canoes have arrived. What a crowd of painted fiends! I get surrounded, and have no way of escape. Sticks and spears rattle round. I get a knock on the head, and a piece of stick falls on my hand. My old Lavao friend gets hold of me and walks me to outskirt. Arua and Lauma of Lolo assure me they will not ascend the hill, and we had better not interfere with them. "Right, friend; but you must stop, and on no account injure my friend Kone." It would frighten them were we to go armed to the village; but then we dare not stay here twenty-four hours after. I can do more for the natives unarmed. I am glad I am able to mix with both parties; it shows they mean us no harm, and speaks well for the future. No one was killed, but several were severely wounded, and a few houses destroyed. They have made peace at last, and I have had a meeting in the village with all; the Loloans have promised to be quiet. I told them we could not stay if they were to be constantly threatening. In the afternoon the chiefs came up, and I promised to visit them all. My head aches a little. Had I been killed, I alone should have been to blame, and not the natives. The Delena natives say: "Well, Tamate, had you not been here, many of us would have been killed, and the remainder gone to Naara, never to return." There is some pleasure in being of a little use even to savages.

The next Sunday we had a splendid service. All the young fellows dressed for it by painting their faces. It was amusing and interesting to hear them interpret all I said from Motuan into Loloan; and when I attempted to use a Lolo word, they corrected me if I wrongly pronounced or misplaced it. After service we had all the children and young men to school. A goodly number have got a pretty fair hold of letters. Some would beat native cloth, and Kone grew very angry, and, because they would not listen to him, threatened to pull up his recently buried child. I sent word that he must on no account do that, and must say no more to the men beating cloth; that by-and-by the people will become enlightened, and then they will understand the Sabbath. Poor Kone's idea is that now and at once they should understand.

On June 6th, I once more left Delena to proceed to Maiva, and, although a heavy sea was running at the time, landed safely about eleven a.m. at Miria's village, on the Maiva coast. I saw a number of people with *karevas* (long fighting sticks), and wondered what was the matter. I said to my old friend Rua, who met me on the beach, "Are you going to fight?" "No, no; it is all right now." I gave him a large axe for Meauri and party to cut wood for a house at their village. Meauri and a number of followers soon made their appearance: it seemed strange that they should have come down so soon. Miria, the chief, being away cutting wood, went to Meauri's village, passing through several seaside villages. We selected a new position for the house, at the back of a large temple; gave them tobacco and red cloth, they promising gladly to have wood cut against my next return. Sitting on the platform, Rua turned to me and asked, "Tamate, who is your real Maiva friend?" Fancying there was trouble, I replied, "Oa Maoni, who sleeps in that house in death, was my friend: Meauri, Rua, Paru, and Aua are now my friends." "I thought so, and Miria has no business to build a house for you. Before we saw the boat we were down on the beach at Miria's village to begin a quarrel; we saw you were coming, and we waited for you." "But I want a house on the coast as well as inland; Miria's village is small and too exposed, and I must look for another place." "That is all right; but this first." "Be it so." After visiting three villages I had not seen before, and going through all the inland ones, I returned to Miria's village; he not having returned, I went along to Ereere. After dark, Miria came in. He felt sorry when I told him I could not put a house up in his place, owing to its being exposed to south-east wind, and to there not being many people. "But I have cut the wood." "I shall pay you for that, and the wood can remain for my return." I gave him tobacco for the young men and a present to himself, and all was right.

A few mornings later, I found the natives sitting round rice; one said, "Come, we are waiting for you to bless the food." They have seen our boats' crews of Botu and Boera natives always asking a blessing. I said to them, "Cannot one of you ask a blessing?"

"No; wait until we learn, and you will see." A good story is told by the captain of the *Mayri*. On their going to Aroma to relieve the teachers after the Kalo massacre, in the early morning they were pulling along the reef, and just as the sun appeared over the mountains, one of the Motu crew called on all to be quiet, rowers to lean on their oars, and then engaged in prayer, thanking God for watching over them during the night, and praying that He would care for them during the day, and that no unpleasantness might occur with the Aroma natives. All along this coast, and right away down to Elema as far as Bald Head, the Motu tribe has a wonderful influence, and in a few years excellent pioneers may be had from it. They must have been a terrible lot in the past. I have heard much from themselves of piracy, murder, and robbery, and all along here they tell terrible tales. A Motu chief in one of our meetings, speaking of the past and the present, concluded by saying: "Since the arrival of the foreigners (teachers), we have changed and will continue to change."

An old chief, Aiio, from the Mekeo district, came in to see me, and brought me as a present a splendid head-dress, which is hung up by Kone in front of the tent for all to see. On giving him a present of salt, it was pleasant to see the old fellow's expression of pleasure. He is anxious I should go inland as soon as possible; I tell him I must wait for tomahawks.

At seven o'clock on the morning of the 13th of June, I started to visit Madu, the chief of the Motu Lavao. We went up from the bight, a large saltwater creek, with dense mangrove on both banks,—a veritable bed of fever,—and anchoring our boats, we walked through the deserted village of Paitana and on for about a mile and a half to Motu Lavao. The path leads along a narrow tract of good country, with dense swamps on both sides. The village is large, with good houses kept nice and clean; but I can conceive of no more unhealthy locality—swamp all around. A number of people were down with fever, some in their houses, others lying exposed to the sun. I asked them if they had no *vatavata* (spirits) knocking around in their district, and did they not much trouble them. "Oh, trouble us much, very much." I told them I thought so, and the sooner they removed from that place the better—that they were right in the centre of sickness and death. They said, "And what is to become of the place of our forefathers, and the cocoanuts they planted?" "Better leave them, or in a short time there will be none left to remember their forefathers, or eat their cocoanuts." Madu was in the country, and we waited his return. He tried hard to get me to stay over-night, but it was of no use. He presented me with a pig and feathers, and we concluded friendship by my giving a return present. An old woman was presented to me, a great sorceress; but, not liking the sisterhood, I did not see my way clear to give her a present. Such as she keep the natives in constant fear, do what they like, and get what they like. It is affirmed by all that the great Lolo sorcerer, Arua, keeps snakes in bamboos, and uses them for his nefarious purposes. Late in the afternoon we left, accompanied by Madu and a number of youths carrying pig, cocoanuts, and sugar-cane. When leaving, the chief said, "Go, Tamate; we are friends."

On June 14th, I had a long conference with the old Paitana chief, Boutu, and his followers. They looked very much excited and alarmed when I met them, but that wore away during our conversation. Boutu, his party, and other Lolo natives assured me that the attack on Dr. James and Mr. Thorngren was unknown to all but those in the canoe. The excuse was that the day before they were trading on Yule Island one young man had feathers for sale. Dr. James and Waunaea told him to leave; they would not take his feathers because he objected to the pearl shell produced. This, they say, was the beginning. He tried very hard to sell his feathers, and, if possible, get a tomahawk. Failing, he went home, quietly arranged a party, slept in the bush, and before daylight went off to the vessel. On nearing the vessel, Dr. James called out—"You must not come alongside: you are coming to kill me." They said, "We are not going to kill you, but want to sell yams." The yams were taken on board, and whilst Dr. James was counting the beads to pay for them he was struck with a club, and afterwards speared, but not quite disabled, as he drew his revolver and shot the man who attacked him. Mr. Thorngren was struck at from aft, fell overboard, and was never again seen. They say, when the people in the village heard of it, they were very sorry, and that ever since they have been looked upon with anger, as they have been the cause of keeping the white man away with his tobacco, beads, and tomahawks. I asked them, "What now?" "Let us make friends, and never again have the like." "But your young men could do the same again without your knowing." "They know better than try it again; they are too much afraid; and they see that what was then done has greatly injured us as well as all the other villages." I explained to them the object of our coming here, and that they must not think we are to buy everything they bring, and must not be angry when we refuse to give what they demand. We do not come to steal their food or curios, and, if we do not want them, they can carry all back; we are not traders. After praying with them, they said, "Tamate, now let it be friendship; give up your intention of going to Mekeo (inland district), and come to-morrow, and we shall make friends and peace." "I shall go; but suppose the mother of the young man who was shot begins wailing, what then?" "She will doubtless wail, but you need not fear; come, and you will see." "Then to-morrow I shall go."

Next morning, the *Mayri* having arrived the evening before, I carried into effect the intended visit. The chief of Paitana and two followers, with my friend Lauma, of Lolo, waited to accompany me. After breakfast we got into the boat, Lavao in charge. We entered the same creek as for Motu Lavao, and when up it some distance turned up another to the right, too narrow to use oars. When two miles up we anchored boat, then walked or waded for two miles through swamp and long grass. When near the village we heard loud wailing, and Lavao, who was leading, thought it better we should wait for the old chief, who was some distance behind. On coming up they spoke in Lolo, then threw down his club, calling on one of his followers to pick it up. He went in front, and called on me to follow close to him, the others coming after; and so we marched into the village and up on to his platform. Then began speechifying, presenting cooked food, betel-nuts, pig, and feathers. When all was finished I gave my present, and said a few words in the Motu dialect. The uncle of the man shot by Dr. James came on to the platform, caught me by the arm and shouted, *Maino*! (peace), saying that they, the chiefs, knew nothing of the attack. The murderers lived at the other end of the village; and thither, accompanied by a large party, I went. They gave me a pig, and I gave them a return present. The real murderer of Mr. Thorngren sat near me, dressed for the occasion, and four others who were in the canoe stood near the platform. The mother and two widows were in the house opposite, but with good sense refrained from wailing. I spoke to them of the meanness and treachery of attacking as they attacked Dr. James and Mr. Thorngren. They say there were ten in the canoe—one was shot, three have since died, and six remain. They also say they feel they have done wrong, as they not only made the foreigners their enemies, but also all the tribes around were angry with them. "What now, then?" "Oh, *maino* (peace) it must be; we are friends, and so are all foreigners now." "I am not a trader, but have come to teach about the only one true God and His love to us all in the gift of His Son Jesus Christ, to proclaim peace between man and man, and tribe and tribe." What seemed to astonish them most was my being alone and unarmed. After some time, our old friend came from the other end of the village and hurried us away. It was time to leave them, so, giving a few parting presents, we picked up our goods and away to the boat.

CHAPTER V
EAST CAPE IN 1878 AND IN 1882

Original state of the natives—War and cannibalism—How the mission work has been carried on—A Sunday at East Cape in 1882—Twenty-one converts baptized—A blight prospect.

In 1878, missionary work was begun at East Capes, and four years after the establishment of that mission, on a review of the past, what evidences of progress were to be seen! There were signs of light breaking in upon the long dark night of heathenism. Looking at the condition of this people when the missionaries and teachers first landed, what did they find? A people sunk in crime that to them has become a custom and religion—a people in whom murder is the finest art, and who from their earliest years study it. Disease, sickness, and death have all to be accounted for. They know nothing of malaria, filth, or contagion. Hence they hold that an enemy causes these things, and friends have to see that due punishment is made. The large night firefly helps to point in the direction of that enemy, or the spirits of departed ones are called in through spiritists' influence to come and assist, and the medium pronouncing a neighbouring tribe guilty, the time is near when that tribe will be visited and cruel deeds done. They know nothing of a God of Love—only gods and spirits who are ever revengeful, and must be appeased; who fly about in the night and disturb the peace of homes. It is gross darkness and cruelty, brother's hand raised against brother's. Great is the chief who claims many skulls; and the youth, who may wear a jawbone as an armlet is to be admired.

When we first landed here, the natives lived only to fight, and the victory was celebrated by a cannibal feast. It is painfully significant to find that the only field in which New Guinea natives have shown much skill and ingenuity is in the manufacture of weapons. One of these is known as a Man-catcher, and was invented by the natives of Hood Bay, but all over the vast island this loop of rattan cane is the constant companion of head-hunters. The peculiarity of the weapon is the deadly spike inserted in the handle.

The *modus operandi* is as follows:—The loop is thrown over the unhappy wretch who is in retreat, and a vigorous pull from the brawny arm of the vengeful captor jerks the victim upon the spike, which (if the weapon be deftly handled) penetrates the body at the base of the brain, or, if lower down, in the spine, in either case inflicting a death-wound.

All these things are changed, or in process of change. For several years there have been no cannibal ovens, no desire for skulls. Tribes that could not formerly meet but to fight, now meet as friends, and sit side by side in the same house worshipping the true God. Men and women who, on the arrival of the mission, sought the missionaries' lives, are only anxious now to do what they can to assist them, even to the washing of their feet. How the change came about is simply by the use of the same means as those acted upon in many islands of the Pacific. The first missionaries landed not only to preach the Gospel of Divine love, but also to live it, and to show to the savage a more excellent way than theirs. Learning the language, mixing freely with them, showing kindnesses, receiving the same, travelling with them, differing from them, making friends, assisting them in their trading, and in every way making them feel that their good only was sought. They thought at first that we were compelled to leave our own land because of hunger!

Teachers were placed amongst the people; many sickened and died. There was a time of great trial, but how changed is everything now! Four years pass on, and, in 1882, we visit them. We left Port Moresby, and arrived at East Cape on a Sunday. Morning service was finished, and, from the vessel, we saw a number of natives well dressed, standing near the mission house, waiting to receive us. The teachers came off, and with them several lads, neatly dressed. After hearing from them of the work, and of how the people were observing the Sabbath, we landed, and were met by a quiet, orderly company of men, women, and boys, who welcomed us as real friends. The first to shake hands with us was a chief from the opposite side of the bay, who in early days gave us much trouble, and had to be well watched. Now he was dressed, and his appearance much altered. It was now possible to meet him and feel he was a friend. We found Pi Vaine very ill, and not likely to live long; yet she lived long enough to rejoice in the glorious success of the Gospel of Christ, and to see many of those for whom she laboured profess Christianity. We were astonished, when we met in the afternoon, at the orderly service—the nice well-tuned singing of hymns, translated by the teacher, and the attention, when he read a chapter in Mark's Gospel—translated by him from the Rarotongan into the dialect of the place. When he preached to them, all listened attentively, and seemed to be anxious not to forget a single word. Two natives prayed with great earnestness and solemnity. After service all remained, and were catechised on the sermon, and then several present stood up and exhorted their friends to receive the Gospel. Many strangers were present, and they were exhorted to come as often as possible and hear the good news. Then, again, others offered prayers. We found that numbers came in on the Saturday with food and cooking-pots, and remained until Monday morning. They lived with the teachers, and attended all the services, beginning with a prayer-meeting on Saturday night.

During our stay of a few days, they all remained at the station, and we saw much of them. The teachers said there were twenty-one who professed faith in Christ and had given up heathenism and desired baptism. We visited further on to the east, and we were a week away on our return to East Cape, and after close examination of each candidate we decided to baptize them on the following Tuesday. The service was most interesting, and well attended by persons from various places. At night we examined the children and grown-up people who attend school, and were much pleased with them. A few can read in the Motu dialect; others know how to put letters together and form words. We hope soon to have one or two books in their own dialect. Of those baptized several are anxious to be instructed, that they may be better fitted to do work for Christ amongst their own countrymen. Already they hold services, and exhort in other villages, and when travelling they do all the good they can to others.

We are in hopes soon to receive a number of young men and women at Port Moresby, and begin our Institution, to be called "The

New Guinea Institution for Training Evangelists." At present we shall proceed quickly, building native houses for students, and a class room to be bought in the colonies, towards which our true friends in North Adelaide contribute largely.

The harvest ripens fast: where shall we look for labourers? The Master has said, "Pray." May they soon be sent! The light is shining, the darkness is breaking, and the thick clouds are moving, and the hidden ones are being gathered in. We have already plucked the first flowers; stern winter yields, and soon we shall have the full spring, the singing of birds, and the trees in full blossom. Hasten it, O Lord, we plead!

CPSIA information can be obtained
at www.ICGtesting.com
Printed in the USA
BVHW031705280621
610633BV00004B/960

9 789354 753008